Winning through Strategic Prayer

WARFARE
of an Intercessor

Sabrina A. Smith

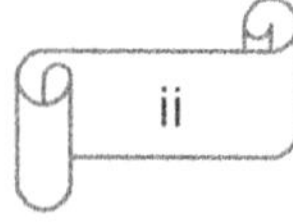

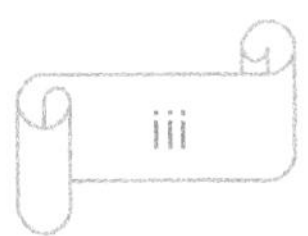

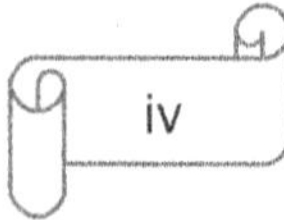

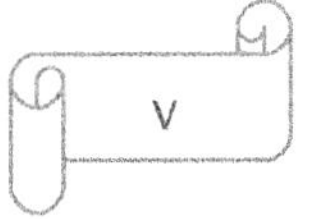
V

Book Cover

I want to pause here to acknowledge the story behind the book cover.

While the artwork was created by a graphic artist, this was her first time designing a book cover, although she creates and makes banners, prophetic art, etc. We began with conversations sharing the heart of the message and the imagery I carried, particularly the vision of the sword. From there, the rest of the design unfolded through her discernment and creativity. What appears on the cover is not merely design, it is interpretation.

I am grateful for the way God entrusted the remaining vision to her hands.

Thank you, **Prophetess Ingrid Ortiz**, owner of **Heavens Expressions**, for stewarding what was shared and allowing the Spirit to shape what could not be explained in words alone.

A Word About the Book Cover

Before moving further into the language of warfare, it is important to pause and understand what is already being communicated without words.

This cover is not decorative. It is declarative.

At the center is the sword, drawn from the account of Eleazar, one of David's mighty warriors. Scripture records that *"he arose and attacked the Philistines until his hand was weary, and his hand stuck to the sword"* **(2 Samuel 23:10, NKJV)**. Eleazar did not disengage when strength diminished. He remained when fatigue set in. And it was there at the point of weariness that the Lord brought about a great victory.

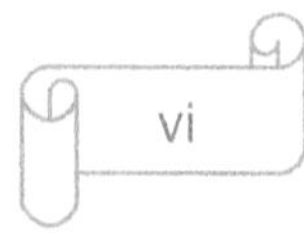

This detail matters. His hand was weary, but it did not release the sword.

The sword represents the Word of God not as concept, but as weapon. It speaks to the intercessor who has learned that victory is not secured by intensity alone, but by persistence in truth. There are moments in warfare when strength wanes, endurance is tested, and prayer feels costly. In those moments, what matters most is not how forcefully one strikes, but whether one holds fast to what God has spoken.

The sword pinned into the ground on the cover is intentional. It symbolizes finality. It declares that the battle has already been decided. The sword is not raised in uncertainty; it is planted in victory. This image echoes the finished work of Christ it is finished and affirms that the intercessor does not fight for triumph, but from it.

Surrounding the sword is fire.

Fire in Scripture represents the sustaining presence of God. The Lord commanded that *"the fire on the altar shall be kept burning... it shall not go out"* **(Leviticus 6:12–13, NKJV)**. This was not chaotic fire, but ordered fire maintained through obedience rather than effort. It reveals that holy fire is meant to remain without consuming the one who tends it.

This same truth is seen when Moses encountered the burning bush *"the bush was burning with fire, but the bush was not consumed"* **(Exodus 3:2, NKJV).** God's fire does not destroy what He chooses to dwell in. It refines, empowers, and remains. For the intercessor, the fire on the cover speaks of consecration, authority, and divine presence sustained over time.

Rising from the fire is smoke.

In Scripture, smoke signifies offering and intercession before God. The psalmist prayed, *"Let my prayer be set before You as incense, the lifting up of my hands as the evening sacrifice"* **(Psalm 141:2,**

NKJV). Smoke rising upward testifies that prayer does not fall to the ground ascends.

The book of Revelation confirms this image, describing how *"the smoke of the incense, with the prayers of the saints, ascended before God"* **(Revelation 8:3–4, NKJV)**. What is offered at the altar is received, remembered, and acted upon. Smoke represents prayers that linger, intercession that continues to speak even when words grow quiet.

Together, the sword, the fire, and the smoke tell one unified story.

This is the posture of the intercessor:
holding fast to the Word when weary,
standing in victory already secured,
remaining at the altar while prayer ascends.

God moves on behalf of those who remain aligned.
Victory is enforced by those who do not withdraw.
Endurance anchored in truth always advances purpose.

This book is written for those whose hands may be tired
but whose grip on the Word remains unbroken.

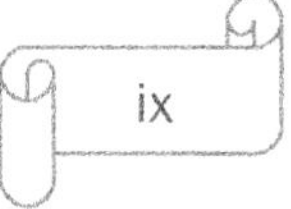
ix

Table of Contents

Foreword

Warfare of an Intercessor: Winning Through Strategic Prayer was written for those who have learned that intercession is not sustained by intensity alone. Throughout Scripture, spiritual warfare is revealed as ordered, governed, and intentionally not reactive or chaotic. Many who are called to apostolic and prophetic intercession have discovered that the warfare they endured was not incidental, but strategic. It was an assignment of resistance designed to silence prayer, disrupt governance, and prevent the exercise of spiritual authority. Scripture consistently affirms this reality: *"For we do not wrestle against flesh and blood, but against principalities, against powers, against the rulers of the darkness of this age"* **(Ephesians 6:12, NKJV)**.

God Himself acknowledged this kind of opposition when He commissioned Jeremiah *"to root out and to pull down, to destroy and to throw down, to build and to plant"* **(Jeremiah 1:10, NKJV)**, revealing that authority attracts resistance. Jesus warned Peter, *"Simon, Simon! Indeed, Satan has asked for you, that he may sift you as wheat"* (Luke 22:31, NKJV). This exposes how assignment draws targeted attack and how Daniel's prolonged intercession revealed that answers may be delayed not by God's silence, but by unseen warfare, for *"the prince of the kingdom of Persia withstood me twenty-one days"* **(Daniel 10:13, NKJV)**.

Trauma, disappointment, fear, unbelief, broken relationships, and seasons of loss were not merely personal trials; they were attempts to hinder those entrusted with influence from standing, ruling, and remaining aligned. This book does not call intercessors to pray harder, but to pray wiser, to understand assignment, to steward authority, and remain aligned with Heaven's purpose over time. From early battles to mature governance, these pages trace the formation of an intercessor whose warfare produces lasting impact, whose authority endures, and whose prayers help establish what God intends to remain in the earth.

INTRODUCTION

A Summons to the Intercessor

This is more than a call to prayer.
It is a summons to spiritual warfare.

Before I ever understood prayer, warfare had already found me. I was born early in entrance (prematurely) into a world that did not yet know my name, but the enemy recognized my destiny. Long before I could articulate purpose, opposition had already been assigned. Trauma followed. Sexual violation of molestation attempted to mark what God had already consecrated, but I'm reminded of the scripture from **Jeremiah 1:10 (NKJV)** *"Before I formed you in the womb, I knew you, before you were born, I sanctified you, I ordained you a prophet to the nations"*

What I did not understand then, I now recognize clearly: The enemy does not fight what carries no threat.

Scripture tells us that God knows us before we are formed in the womb. If heaven marks us early, then hell resists us early. The womb becomes the first battlefield, and destiny becomes the target. Many of us survived battles we could not name, until God opened our eyes and called us into intercession. Long before we were trained, we were targeted. Long before we understood authority, we were contending. God did not call us into prayer to introduce us to conflict; He called us to give language, structure, and strategy to the wars we had already endured. Intercession is not a new assignment, it is the divine interpretation of our history, revealing that every preserved life was and is a testimony of victory in motion.

Warfare of an Intercessor is written for those who sense that their prayer life was forged through fire, for those who have felt resistance before revelation, and for those who know deep in their spirit that prayer is not passive. It is militant. It is strategic. It is authoritative.

Spiritual warfare is not emotional striving or fear-driven engagement; it is a disciplined campaign strateia and for many, it is not occasional, but vocational. Scripture presents warfare as an apostolic career, a sustained and intentional assignment carried out from a place of victory, not defeat. We do not fight to obtain triumph; we fight from the triumph Christ has already secured.

In its literal sense, strateia(warfare) refers to military service, a campaign, or an expedition. In the New Testament, it describes the active, ongoing work of the believer, particularly those called apostolically as a soldier's campaign marked by discipline, endurance, resistance, and direct confrontation with spiritual opposition.

Apostolic life is not passive devotion but active advancement, waging war against forces that oppose the kingdom of God.

This calling includes proclaiming the gospel, establishing and strengthening the Church, guarding truth, and standing firm amid persecution and trial. Practically, this apostolic warfare is expressed through persistent prayer and intercession, perseverance through hardship, disciplined focus on divine assignment, bold proclamation, sacrificial service, and intentional community building.

2 Corinthians 10:3–5 (NKJV)

"For though we walk in the flesh, we do not war according to the flesh. For the weapons of our warfare (strateias) are not carnal but mighty in God for pulling down strongholds, casting down arguments and every high thing that exalts itself against the knowledge of God."

Commissioning Declaration for Apostolic Intercessors

I acknowledge that I have not been called to passive prayer, but to apostolic warfare.

I receive my assignment as one sent
sent to stand in the gap,
sent to confront spiritual resistance,
sent to advance the purposes of God in the earth.

I declare that my warfare is disciplined, ordered, and victorious.
I do not fight from fear or emotion,
but from the authority secured through Christ Jesus.
The weapons of my warfare are not carnal,
but mighty in God for the pulling down of strongholds.

I embrace *strateia* as my calling
a sustained campaign of prayer, truth, endurance, and obedience.
I endure hardship as a good soldier of Jesus Christ,
unentangled from distractions,
focused on the mission entrusted to me.

I renounce silence, compromise, and retreat.
I take my place as a watchman, a builder, and a warrior.
I proclaim truth, establish righteousness,
and labor until God's will is done on earth as it is in heaven.

I submit to Christ as my Commander,
to the Holy Spirit as my Strategist,
and to the Word of God as my rule of engagement.

I am commissioned to war wisely,
to intercede effectively,
and to stand faithfully until victory is made visible.

I am not merely called to pray.
I am commissioned to advance.

In the name of Jesus Christ,
Amen.

Reader Reflection: Responding to the Apostolic Call

(Journal or meditate prayerfully)

Take a moment to sit quietly before the Lord. Read the commissioning declaration again, slowly. Let each phrase settle in your spirit, not as theory, but as invitation.

Reflect on the following:

1. In what ways have I viewed prayer as occasional rather than vocational?
   How does understanding warfare as a sustained apostolic assignment shift my perspective?

2. Where have I been engaging in spiritual battles emotionally instead of strategically?
   What would it look like to war from a place of victory rather than striving?

3. Are there areas where I have felt resistance, opposition, or unusual pressure that may be connected to my calling rather than my weakness?

4. What distractions, fears, or compromises might be entangling me and weakening my focus as a soldier of Christ?

5. If I truly believe I am sent, how should that change how I pray, speak, and show up in spiritual spaces?

As you reflect on this calling, understand this: warfare, in this sense, is not a moment, it is a mandate. It is not reserved for a select few, nor limited to those who feel fully prepared. It unfolds over time, through obedience, training, and surrender. Whether you are a seasoned intercessor or just awakening to your role, *Warfare of an Intercessor* is designed to equip you to:

- **Discern spiritual warfare accurately** identifying patterns of opposition, timing of attacks, and the enemy's strategies without becoming distracted or fearful.

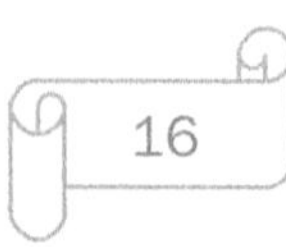

- **Wage war from a place of victory**, enforcing Christ's finished work rather than striving for breakthrough through human effort.

- **Pray strategically and apostolically**, aligning intercession with Heaven's blueprint and praying with precision, authority, and endurance.

- **Pull down strongholds and dismantle lies**, confronting spiritual resistance that opposes identity, truth, and the advancement of God's Kingdom.

- **Stand firm through prolonged battles**, remaining anchored in faith, discipline, and obedience when warfare is intense or delayed.

- **Guard and steward your calling**, avoiding burnout, emotional entanglement, and spiritual distraction while remaining focused on divine assignment.

- **Build and strengthen spiritual territory**, establishing God's will in families, communities, and the Body of Christ through sustained intercession.

- **Respond to warfare as a mandate**, not a moment, embracing prayer as an ongoing apostolic assignment rather than an occasional response.

This book is not about glorifying battles, it is about exposing strategy, enforcing Christ's victory, and raising disciplined intercessors who understand their authority in the spirit.

Prepare to be awakened.
Prepare to be empowered.
Prepare to be equipped.

The battlefield is real.
The warriors are rising.
And Heaven is waiting on the intercessor.

I encourage you to engage with the Reader Reflection and pen your own experiences and allow Holy Spirit to minister to your heart concerning the matter.

Chapter 1: Born Into Battle

The womb as the first battlefield. Long before language is formed, before identity is consciously understood, and before purpose is publicly revealed, spiritual warfare often begins. Scripture makes clear that the womb is not merely a biological space, it is a sacred and spiritual one. It is where God forms, marks, and assigns destiny (Jeremiah 1:5) Because of this, it often becomes the first place of resistance.

God does not wait until adulthood to establish purpose. He begins in hidden places, forming destiny in secrecy, beyond human awareness. And where God is intentional, the enemy becomes observant. The enemy cannot create destiny, but he can attempt to interrupt, distort, or delay what God has already declared.

This is why many battles begin early sometimes even before birth. Premature birth, early trauma, instability, rejection, or vulnerability are often not random events, but points where resistance attempts to gain access. The womb becomes a battlefield not because it is weak, but because it is sacred. What is formed there matters greatly in the spirit.

Before I learned how to pray, I was already in a war I entered this world prematurely, early, unexpected, fragile in the eyes of man. My mother gave birth to me at seven months, before my body had fully prepared for life outside the womb. At that stage, vital systems are still developing: the lungs are learning how to breathe independently, the brain is still forming delicate connections, the immune system has not yet received its full covering, and even basic functions like feeding and temperature regulation require support. Premature birth carries real risk because the body is asked to survive before it is naturally ready. Fragility is not theoretical at that stage; it is lived.

And yet, I lived.

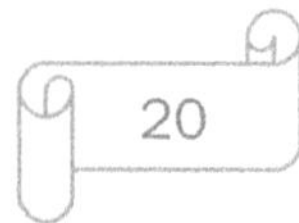

Survival in such conditions is never incidental. It is evidence of preservation. While medicine can explain the risks, it cannot explain purpose. To endure when the body was not yet equipped is more than resilience, it is intervention. Looking back, I understand that my life began in a contested space. The womb, meant to be a place of formation, became my first battlefield. What should have been hidden and protected was instead exposed early. But even there, God sustained me. Fragility did not disqualify me; it marked me. Preservation became the first testimony that my life would be governed not by limitation, but by divine intention.

By every natural measure, my arrival was rushed, unplanned, and vulnerable. Doctors saw risk; Heaven saw purpose. What appeared to be an interruption in the natural was, in truth, a divine appointment in the spirit. I was small yet preserved, early yet sustained. What man labeled fragile; God labeled protected.

My life began as a testimony that survival itself is often the first evidence of calling. But Heaven does nothing prematurely. What appeared early in the natural was right on time in the spirit. I now understand that my early arrival was not random; it was a signal. Destiny had announced itself, and opposition responded.

Scripture consistently affirms that human life is formed, known, and sustained by God, even when circumstances appear incomplete or interrupted. Premature birth, while medically defined as an early entrance into the world, does not indicate divine absence or error. Biblically, God's creative work is not constrained by natural timelines, and His purposes are not nullified by human vulnerability.

Psalm 138:8 declares that the *Lord "will perfect that which concerns" His people"*, affirming that what appears unfinished in the natural remains fully secured in God's sovereign care. Similarly, Isaiah 46:3–4 reveals a God who carries His people "from the womb," emphasizing divine preservation from the earliest stages of life. These passages challenge the assumption that fragility equates to abandonment; rather, they testify that God often reveals His sustaining power most clearly in moments of apparent weakness.

Throughout Scripture, divine calling frequently precedes visible strength. Jeremiah was sanctified before formation (Jeremiah 1:5), and the Apostle Paul testifies that God's strength is made perfect in weakness (2 Corinthians 12:9). In this theological framework, premature birth can be understood not as a disruption of purpose, but as a context in which God's preserving grace is magnified. Preservation itself becomes a sign of divine intention.

From a spiritual warfare perspective, early vulnerability does not signify defeat, but rather highlights the reality that destiny is often contested before it is fully revealed. Yet Scripture affirms that no opposing force can overturn what God has ordained (Job 42:2). Divine preservation stands as both a protective act and a prophetic declaration: what God has formed, He will sustain; what He has purposed, He will complete.

Jeremiah 1:5 (NKJV)
"Before I formed you in the womb I knew you;
Before you were born, I sanctified you;
I ordained you a prophet to the nations."

Many people do not recognize that spiritual warfare does not begin when we are saved, it often begins before we are aware. God marks purpose early, and the enemy studies that purpose just as early. Where destiny is identified, resistance is deployed.

The womb is often the first battlefield.

Psalm 139:13–16 (NKJV)
"For You formed my inward parts;
You covered me in my mother's womb...
All the days fashioned for me,
When as yet there were none of them."

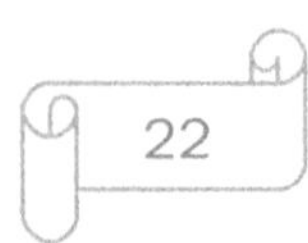

Throughout Scripture, we see that calling precedes conflict. Jeremiah was known before formation. John the Baptist leapt in his mother's womb at the presence of Jesus. Samson's assignment was announced before his birth. The enemy does not fight randomly, he targets what has already been announced in the spirit. Even in Revelation, we see the enemy positioned to devour promise before it could mature (Revelation 12:4). These patterns reveal a sobering truth: destiny is often contested before it is understood.

Early vulnerability does not indicate early defeat. In fact, preservation is often the first evidence of purpose.

Isaiah 46:3–4 (NKJV)
"you have been borne by Me from birth,
Even from the womb…
I will carry you."

My own life bears witness to this truth. Trauma attempted to interrupt purpose at an early stage. Violation sought to distort identity before it could be firmly rooted. Confusion tried to overshadow calling and replace clarity with doubt. These experiences were not isolated or accidental; they were coordinated efforts to wound destiny before it reached maturity.

Molestation, confusion, and shame were not merely emotional injuries, they were calculated spiritual attacks designed to silence my voice before it could be raised with authority. As a child, I was molested repeatedly, and I carried shame like a second skin. It clung to me silently, shaping how I saw myself and how I believed others saw me. Shame did not always speak loudly; often it whispered, convincing me to shrink, to hide, to stay quiet. It taught me to internalize responsibility for what was never mine to bear and to believe that my voice was unwanted or unwelcome.

That shame became a covering I did not choose yet felt unable to remove. It followed me into rooms, into relationships, into my thoughts. While the wounds themselves were unseen, their influence was constant. Shame distorted my identity before I ever had language for who I was created to be. It attempted to convince me that silence was safer than truth and that concealment was protection.

What I understand now is that shame was never just an emotional response, it was a strategy. The enemy sought not only to wound my body, but to imprison my voice and my identity. If he could convince me to remain silent, he could delay purpose. If he could bury identity beneath shame, he could obstruct calling. But even then, God was present. Though I carried shame, shame did not carry authority. Preservation was already at work, even in the places I did not yet recognize as battlegrounds.

The enemy does not assault identity without intention. He targets what threatens him most. Violation works to fracture identity, confusion clouds purpose, and shame presses destiny into secrecy and silence. These strategies are deliberate weapons aimed at muting authority before they can fully emerge.

In Scripture, shame is consistently used as a tool to silence God's people and disconnect them from their identity and authority. Unlike guilt, which convicts behavior, shame attacks being. It whispers that one is unworthy, disqualified, or permanently marked by past experiences. This is why shame is such a powerful weapon in spiritual warfare, it does not merely wound; it attempts to erase voice and visibility.

From the beginning, shame was used to drive Adam and Eve into hiding (Genesis 3:7–10). Though sin had occurred, God sought restoration; yet shame compelled them toward silence and concealment. Similarly, the enemy uses shame to push believers out of alignment with their calling, convincing them that their voice has no authority, and their testimony has no value.

Isaiah 61 reveals God's direct response to shame: restoration, replacement, and commissioning. God does not merely remove shame; He exchanges it for glory (Isaiah 61:7). Where shame silences, redemption restores voice. Where shame hides, healing sends. In this way, shame is exposed not as a permanent condition, but as a defeated strategy when confronted by the redemptive work of Christ.

Isaiah 61:1 (NKJV)
*"The Spirit of the Lord God is upon Me,
Because the Lord has anointed Me
To preach good tidings to the poor;
He has sent Me to heal the brokenhearted,
To proclaim liberty to the captives,
And the opening of the prison to those who are bound."*

What the enemy intended to use as a prison, Christ entered as a liberator. Jesus did not merely come to comfort pain, He came to unbind hearts, expose lies and restore voices. Shame says, "Be quiet." Jesus says, "Proclaim liberty." Confusion says, "You are broken." Jesus says, "You are anointed." Violation attempts to rewrite identity, but redemption restores the original design.

This is why trauma often precedes calling. The enemy attempts to silence intercessors early because he recognizes the authority that will eventually flow from their mouths. But Isaiah 61 does not end with healing, it continues with commissioning. Those who are healed become rebuilders. Those who were bound become proclaimers. Those who survived become sent ones.

I now understand that my healing was never meant to end with me. What Jesus bound up in my heart, He empowered me to confront in prayer for others. The very places where the enemy sought to silence me became the wells from which authority now flows. Restoration did not erase the battle—it redeemed it.

What I did not understand then, I now discern clearly: the enemy was not after my pain, he was after my position.

John 10:10 (NKJV)
"The thief does not come except to steal, and to kill, and to

destroy.
I have come that they may have life, and that they may have it
more abundantly."

Many of us survived battles we could not name until God opened our eyes and called us into intercession. Before we understood prayer as warfare, we endured resistance without language, pressure without explanation, and opposition without instruction. We learned how to survive long before we learned how to stand. Only later did revelation bring clarity: what we thought was chaos was conflict, and what we assumed was personal struggle was often spiritual opposition. When God calls us into intercession, He does not introduce warfare, He reveals the warfare we have already survived.

Spiritual warfare is rarely about the moment—it is about the future.

Revelation 12:4 (NKJV)
"...and the dragon stood before the woman who was ready to
give birth,
to devour her Child as soon as it was born."

Being born into battle does not mean being born defeated. It means you were born carrying something worth fighting over. Survival itself is evidence that the war did not succeed. Preservation is proof of purpose. You are not alive by accident. You are alive because God intervened.

Intercessors are often shaped in hidden places, through unseen wars, long before they ever step into public authority. God allows survival to become training. What the enemy meant for destruction, God uses to develop discernment, authority, and compassion. This book is not about rehearsing wounds.
It is about interpreting warfare correctly.

When you understand that your life has always been contested, you stop asking, "Why me?" and start declaring, "I was chosen." You recognize that prayer is not a religious exercise but a response

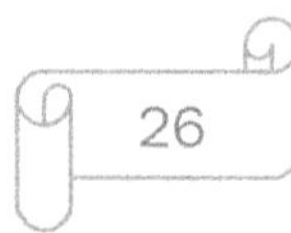

to a lifelong summons. Warfare did not begin when you picked up a prayer strategy, it began when destiny was announced over your life. And now, the same God who preserved you is calling you to stand in the gap for others. You were not just born into battle. You were born to win.

PRAYER DECLARATIONS

- I declare that my life was marked by God before it was contested by the enemy.

- I decree that every early attack against my destiny failed.

- I declare that survival is proof of divine preservation.

- I renounce every false identity formed through trauma and receive God's original design.

- I declare that my past battles have sharpened my discernment, not weakened my faith.

- I accept my call as a governing intercessor and step into warfare with clarity, authority, and confidence.

- I fight from victory, not for victory, through Jesus Christ.

Prayer of Healing and Commissioning

Father God,
I come before You acknowledging that You see fully and heal completely.

I bring every place of trauma, violation, confusion, and shame into Your light.
I declare that these experiences do not define me, silence me, or disqualify me.
Where the enemy attempted to fracture my identity, You have preserved it.
Where shame tried to mute my voice, You have restored authority.

According to Your Word, You bind up the brokenhearted and proclaim liberty to the captives.
So today, I receive healing, not only for what was done to me, but for what the enemy hoped it would stop.

I renounce silence.
I reject false identity.
I release every lie attached to shame.

I receive restoration of voice, clarity of calling, and boldness of purpose.
I declare that my healed places now carry authority.
What was meant to silence me now commissions me.

Send me, Lord, not as one who survived only,
but as one who has been healed, restored, and authorized
to proclaim freedom for others.

In Jesus' name,
Amen.

Prayer:
Lord, help me reinterpret my history through Your truth.
Reveal where You preserved me, protected me, and prepared me.
I receive clarity, healing, and authority as I step into my calling as a governing intercessor. Amen.

READER REFLECTION

(Journal or meditate prayerfully)

1. What battles did I survive before I had language for them?

2. Are there early life experiences I have viewed as personal failure that may have been spiritual opposition?

3. How does knowing that God marked me before birth shift the way I view my past?

4. What evidence of God's preservation can I now identify in my life story?

5. In what ways might God be calling me to intercession through what I have survived?

Chapter 2: Warfare Is a Mandate, Not a Moment

Spiritual warfare is not something the intercessor enters only when trouble arises, it is something the intercessor accepts as an assignment. For many believers, prayer is reactive, activated by crisis, pressure, or fear. But for the intercessor, warfare is not seasonal or situational; it is vocational. It is a mandate.

A moment is temporary.
A mandate is sustained.

Scripture presents warfare not as emotional striving, but as disciplined obedience. The apostle Paul describes warfare using the word *strateia (Greek word for warfare Strongs Greek 4752)*, a campaign, a military service, a sustained engagement. Warfare, in this sense, is not impulsive; it is intentional. It requires structure, endurance, and submission to divine authority.

In spiritual warfare, structure refers to God-ordained order, alignment, and boundaries that govern how warfare is engaged. Biblical warfare is never chaotic, impulsive, or self-directed. Structure ensures that intercession flows from God's command, timing, and strategy rather than human emotion or reaction. Without structure, zeal becomes disorder and passion becomes presumption.

Paul consistently taught that spiritual authority operates within divine order. Structured warfare keeps the intercessor aligned under Christ's headship, grounded in Scripture, and accountable to the Spirit.

Structure allows the intercessor to stand, not scramble - engaging warfare with clarity, restraint, and effectiveness.

1 Corinthians 14:40 (NKJV)
"Let all things be done decently and in order."

Endurance is the capacity to remain faithful, obedient, and spiritually engaged over time, especially when warfare is prolonged and results are delayed. Endurance is not mere survival; it is disciplined perseverance rooted in trust. In apostolic warfare, endurance is essential because many assignments require sustained prayer rather than immediate breakthrough.

Paul presents endurance as a defining mark of spiritual maturity and apostolic calling. Warfare without endurance leads to burnout, retreat, or misdirected frustration.

Endurance teaches the intercessor to trust God's timing while remaining positioned for victory.

Scripture — 2 Timothy 2:3 (NKJV)
"You therefore must endure hardship as a good soldier of Jesus Christ."

Submission to divine authority means that spiritual warfare is never self-appointed or self-directed. The intercessor does not choose battles independently but operates under Christ's lordship and the Holy Spirit's leadership. Authority in warfare flows from submission; apart from it, engagement becomes dangerous and ineffective.

Jesus modeled perfect submission, engaging only what the Father authorized and resisting every temptation to act independently. Likewise, apostolic warfare requires yielding one's will, agenda, and timing to God.

James 4:7 (NKJV)
"Therefore submit to God. Resist the devil and he will flee from you."

John 5:19 (NKJV)
"The Son can do nothing of Himself, but what He sees the Father do."

Spiritual warfare exercised without submission to divine authority is not boldness, it is presumption. Scripture is clear that authority in the spirit does not originate from passion, experience, or volume of prayer, but from alignment under God's command. When warfare is engaged outside of submission, it becomes misdirected, exhausting, and often harmful.

The Bible offers a sobering example in the sons of Sceva (Acts 19:13–16). They attempted to exercise spiritual authority without relationship or submission to Christ, and the result was humiliation and injury. Their error was not acknowledging Jesus' power—it was attempting to use authority they were not submitted to. This passage reveals that spiritual authority cannot be borrowed, imitated, or assumed; it must flow from submission.

Acts 19:15 (NKJV)
"And the evil spirit answered and said, Jesus I know, and Paul I know; but who are you?"

Warfare without submission often manifests as:

- Praying aggressively without discernment

- Fighting battles God never authorized

- Confusing emotional intensity with spiritual authority

- Becoming reactive, defensive, or spiritually exhausted

- Turning warfare inward—against people rather than principalities

James 4:7 establishes the correct order: *"Submit to God. Resist the devil and he will flee."* Resistance without submission has no promise attached to it. Submission is the gateway through which legitimate authority flows.

For the intercessor, submission does not weaken prayer, it governs it. It provides boundaries, timing, and protection. Submission teaches the intercessor when to engage, when to stand, and when to remain silent. Without it, warfare becomes chaotic and costly; with it, warfare becomes effective and sustainable.

2 Corinthians 10:3–4 (NKJV)

"3. For though we walk in the flesh, we do not war according to the flesh. 4. For the weapons of our warfare are not carnal but mighty in God for pulling down strongholds."

Paul's words in 2 Corinthians 10:3–4 explain why sustained obedience often provokes sustained resistance. When Paul states, *"though we walk in the flesh, we do not war according to the flesh,"* he establishes that spiritual warfare is not triggered by human behavior alone, but by spiritual positioning. Intercessors live ordinary lives in the natural, yet they operate under spiritual authority that threatens unseen structures opposing God's will. Resistance, therefore, does not arise randomly, it responds to assignment.

Paul goes further by declaring that "the weapons of our warfare are not carnal but mighty in God for pulling down strongholds." Strongholds represent entrenched systems of thought, spiritual influence, and opposition that resist God's truth and authority. When an intercessor remains obedient over time, they are not merely praying through moments, they are confronting fortified spiritual resistance. Sustained obedience applies sustained pressure to these strongholds, and what is fortified will resist being dismantled.

This is why many intercessors encounter repeated or intensified opposition when they remain faithful to their calling. Resistance is not evidence of misalignment, but often confirmation of effectiveness. Paul's language reveals that warfare intensifies not when believers act emotionally, but when they act consistently.

Carnal weapons, human effort, emotion, or force cannot dismantle spiritual strongholds. But Spirit-led obedience, maintained over time, becomes "mighty in God."

In this way, the scripture reframes resistance. Opposition is not always a sign to retreat; often it is a response to the pressure being applied to spiritual systems that are being challenged. When warfare is understood as a mandate, not a moment, the intercessor no longer interprets resistance as failure, but as indication that the battle is being engaged at the level where real change occurs.

For some, this is often where weariness sets in. Those who believe warfare is only a moment become discouraged when the pressure lasts longer than expected. But those who understand warfare as a mandate learn how to stand, endure, and advance without burnout or confusion.

Paul reinforces this truth when instructing Timothy.

2 Timothy 2:3–4 (NKJV)
"You therefore must endure hardship as a good soldier of Jesus Christ.

No one engaged in warfare entangles himself with the affairs of this life, that he may please him who enlisted him as a soldier."

Endurance is not optional in apostolic warfare it is essential. The intercessor is not called to fight until it becomes uncomfortable, but until the assignment is complete. This requires focus, discipline, and the willingness to remain aligned even when results are delayed.

Understanding warfare as a mandate also brings discernment. When warfare is seen as a lifelong assignment rather than a momentary reaction, the intercessor learns to distinguish between what must be engaged and what must be ignored. Discernment grows through sustained obedience. Instead of responding emotionally to every provocation, the intercessor begins to recognize patterns, timing, and spiritual intent. Mandated warfare trains the believer to hear God's voice clearly in the midst of pressure and to respond according to divine instruction rather than impulse.

Scripture affirms that discernment is cultivated through practice and maturity, not urgency.

Hebrews 5:14 (NKJV)
"But solid food belongs to those who are of full age, that is, those who by reason of use have their senses exercised to discern both good and evil."

Because mandated warfare is sustained, it sharpens spiritual perception over time. The intercessor learns when opposition is an assignment to confront and when it is a distraction meant to derail focus. Discernment protects against misdirected warfare, battles fought in the flesh, prayers offered prematurely, or confrontations God never authorized.

James reinforces this truth by linking discernment to submission and wisdom rather than zeal.

James 1:5 (NKJV)
"If any of you lacks wisdom, let him ask of God, who gives to all liberally and without reproach, and it will be given to him."

Jesus Himself modeled this level of discernment. Though surrounded by constant need and opposition, He did not engage every demand placed upon Him. He moved according to the Father's will, not the crowd's urgency.

John 5:19 (NKJV)
"The Son can do nothing of Himself, but what He sees the Father do."

Understanding warfare as a mandate anchors the intercessor in this same posture. It replaces reaction with revelation and emotion with obedience. Discernment becomes the compass that guides engagement, ensuring that warfare remains effective, lawful, and aligned with Heaven's intent. In this way, discernment is not merely a spiritual gift, it is a byproduct of faithful, submitted warfare.

Not every provocation requires engagement, and not every battle is ours to initiate. Mandated warfare follows Heaven's timing, not emotional urgency. Authority increases when the intercessor learns when to advance and when to remain positioned.

Jesus modeled this perfectly. He did not respond to every accusation, confront every demon, or move at every demand. He moved according to assignment. He prayed consistently, withdrew intentionally, and advanced strategically. His warfare was purposeful, not reactive.

When warfare is understood correctly, frustration gives way to focus. Confusion gives way to clarity. Prayer becomes disciplined rather than desperate. Authority strengthens when the intercessor understands they are sent not scrambling.

This chapter marks a turning point. You are no longer merely identifying warfare; you are accepting responsibility for how you engage it. At this stage, the intercessor moves beyond recognizing opposition and begins to govern their response to it. Warfare is no longer something that simply happens around you, it is something you are entrusted to engage wisely, lawfully, and under divine authority.

Scripture consistently teaches that spiritual maturity is revealed not by awareness alone, but by discerning action. Knowing there is a battle does not automatically mean one is prepared to fight it correctly.

Luke 12:48 (NKJV)
"...For everyone to whom much is given, from him much will be required."

With revelation comes accountability. As God opens the intercessor's eyes to the nature of warfare, He also calls them to greater discipline, restraint, and obedience. Responsibility means choosing when to engage and when to remain still, when to confront and when to cover, and when to advance and when to endure. It is the difference between reacting to opposition and responding under instruction.

Paul emphasizes this transition when he speaks of intentional, governed warfare:

1 Corinthians 9:26–27 (NKJV)
"Therefore I run thus: not with uncertainty. Thus, I fight not as one who beats the air."

Responsible warfare is purposeful. It does not waste energy on unauthorized battles or emotional reactions. It is measured, focused, and aligned with Heaven's strategy. The intercessor learns that not every provocation is an assignment, and not every conflict requires confrontation.

Peter reinforces this call to governed engagement by urging believers to remain sober and watchful:

1 Peter 5:8 (NKJV)
"Be sober, be vigilant, because your adversary the devil walks about like a roaring lion..."

Sobriety and vigilance are marks of responsibility. They require self-control, spiritual alertness, and submission to God's leading. Accepting responsibility for warfare also means guarding one's heart, words, and posture so that authority is not compromised through carelessness or pride.

Ultimately, accepting responsibility transforms the intercessor's posture. Warfare is no longer approached with anxiety or bravado, but with humility and confidence rooted in obedience. The intercessor understands that authority is not proven by how aggressively one fights, but by how accurately one obeys. Warfare, in this sense, is not a moment it is a mandate.

As you close this chapter, take a moment to consider what has shifted within you. Recognizing warfare brings awareness, but accepting responsibility brings maturity.

Declaration

- I declare that I am no longer reactive, but responsible.

- I engage in warfare under divine authority, not human emotion.

- I fight with clarity, discipline, and submission to God's command.

- I do not battle aimlessly or waste spiritual energy.

- I am entrusted with this mandate, and I steward it faithfully.

- I accept responsibility for how I engage warfare.

- I stand aligned with Heaven's will.

Prayer

Father God,

I thank You for opening my eyes to the reality of spiritual warfare. I acknowledge that awareness alone is not enough, I must also steward how I engage what You reveal.

I surrender every reactive pattern, emotional response, and misdirected effort.

Teach me to fight wisely, to stand patiently, and to move only at Your command.
Give me discernment to know when to engage, when to wait, and when to remain silent.

I ask for the grace to carry this mandate with humility and obedience.
Guard my heart, govern my prayers, and align my actions with Your will.

I choose responsibility over reaction and obedience over impulse.

In Jesus' Name
Amen

READER REFLECTION

(Journal or meditate prayerfully)

1. In what ways have I recognized warfare but avoided responsibility for how I engage it?

2. Have I been reacting emotionally to opposition rather than responding under God's direction?

3. Are there battles I have been fighting that God never assigned to me?

4. What does responsible warfare look like in my current season of life?

5. How might my prayer life change if I approached warfare with discipline, discernment, and obedience?

Allow the Holy Spirit to reveal not what condemns, but what clarifies.

Chapter 3: Waging War from Victory
Equipped for Battle

One of the greatest misconceptions in spiritual warfare is the belief that victory is uncertain or still pending. When this misunderstanding takes root, prayer becomes exhausting, urgency turns into anxiety, and intercession is driven more by fear than faith. Yet Scripture consistently declares a different reality: the intercessor does not fight *for* victory; we fight *from* it.

Victory was secured long before we ever stepped onto the battlefield.

Through the cross, Jesus decisively defeated sin, death, and the powers of darkness. His resurrection and exaltation confirmed that the outcome of the war had already been determined. Spiritual warfare today is not about re-winning a battle; it is about enforcing a triumph already established by Christ.

Colossians 2:15 (NKJV)
"Having disarmed principalities and powers, He made a public spectacle of them, triumphing over them in it."

This verse reveals not only Christ's authority, but the enemy's defeat. Principalities and powers were not merely resisted; they were disarmed. Their authority was stripped, their power exposed, and their defeat made public. Intercession, therefore, is not a plea for God to act; it is a partnership with God to enforce what He has already done.

When intercessors forget this truth, prayer subtly shifts into striving. They attempt to generate power through volume, intensity, or repetition. But authority in the Kingdom is never produced by effort—it flows from position.

Paul emphasizes this positional reality when he reminds believers where they are seated.

Ephesians 2:6 (NKJV)
"And raised us up together, and made us sit together in the heavenly places in Christ Jesus."

Seated with Christ does not mean inactive; it means authorized. Position determines perspective. Those who fight from below are easily overwhelmed by what they see. Those who fight from above see resistance in light of victory. When the intercessor understands their position, prayer becomes steadier, clearer, and more confident.

This is why Chapter 3 was essential. Responsibility without victory produces pressure. But responsibility anchored in victory produces authority, endurance, and peace.

The Posture of Standing

Paul's instruction in Ephesians 6 is striking. After listing the armor of God, he repeatedly emphasizes one action: ***stand.***

I've been doing a study of the Postures of Prayers and one of the postures I came across is the posture of standing. I've taught this on my Facebook lives as God instructed me to teach it admonishing the intercessors and prayer warriors to go back to the basic as some have gotten lethargic and complacent in the place of prayer and intercession.

In Scripture, the posture of *standing* is not passive or defensive, it is authoritative. To stand in spiritual warfare means to remain firmly positioned in what God has already established, refusing to be moved by pressure, resistance, or intimidation. Standing is the posture of one who knows the battle has been decided and therefore does not panic, retreat, or strive.

Paul emphasizes this posture repeatedly in Ephesians 6, making it clear that standing is the intercessor's primary response after obedience has been exercised.

Ephesians 6:13 (NKJV)

"...and having done all, to stand."

Standing is not passivity, it is settled confidence. It is the refusal to be moved by intimidation, delay, or resistance. Intercessors who understand victory do not panic when warfare intensifies; they remain positioned. Standing communicates to the enemy that the intercessor is not negotiating, retreating, or uncertain.

Standing also guards the heart. When the outcome is secure, prayer can be sustained without emotional collapse. The intercessor learns to wait without wavering and to enforce truth without anxiety.

In Roman military imagery (which Paul intentionally draws from), soldiers did not stand because they were uncertain, they stood because ground had been taken and must now be held. Standing was a declaration that retreat was not an option.

Spiritually, this means the intercessor:

- does not renegotiate what God has spoken
- does not retreat because resistance intensifies
- does not strive to "do more" when God has already said, *stand*

Standing is faith expressed through restraint.

1 Corinthians 16:13 (NKJV)

"Watch, stand fast in the faith, be brave, be strong."

Psalm 46:10 (NKJV)

"Be still and know that I am God."

Stillness here does not mean inactivity; it means confidence in God's sovereignty.

Weapons of Warfare: Equipped, Not Striving

Waging war from victory does not mean disengaging from battle; it means engaging with proper equipment. Scripture teaches that God has fully equipped the believer for spiritual warfare. The intercessor is never sent uncovered.

Ephesians 6:10–11 (NKJV)
"10. Finally, my brethren, be strong in the Lord and in the power of His might. 11. Put on the whole armor of God, that you may be able to stand against the wiles of the devil."

The armor of God is not merely defensive, it is strategic. Each piece enables the intercessor to remain effective during sustained warfare.

- The belt of truth anchors discernment. Truth keeps prayer aligned with reality rather than emotion. Without truth, warfare becomes exaggerated or misdirected.

- The breastplate of righteousness guards the heart. It protects the intercessor from condemnation, shame, and accusation, common tactics used to weaken authority.

- The shoes of the gospel of peace establish stability. Warfare waged without peace becomes chaotic and reactive. Peace allows the intercessor to move with clarity.

- The shield of faith extinguishes intimidation. Faith absorbs the fiery darts of doubt, fear, and delay, preventing discouragement from taking root.

- The helmet of salvation guards the mind. Identity must be protected, or the intercessor will begin to question their authority and calling.

- The sword of the Spirit—the Word of God is the primary offensive weapon.

Hebrews 4:12 (NKJV)
"For the word of God is living and powerful, and sharper than any two-edged sword..."

The Word of God is not symbolic, it is active. Intercessors do not argue with darkness; they declare Scripture. They do not negotiate with lies; they confront them with truth. The Word executes judgment against falsehood and enforces Heaven's decree on earth.

This is why prayer saturated with Scripture carries authority. Emotional prayer may express desperation, but Word-based prayer enforces dominion.

Paul concludes the armor passage by revealing the environment in which all these weapons operate:

Ephesians 6:18 (NKJV)
"Praying always with all prayer and supplication in the Spirit..."

Prayer is not an accessory to the armor, it is the atmosphere in which it functions. Intercessors remain alert, Spirit-led, and persevering, standing not only for themselves but for others. Warfare from victory requires consistency, not panic.

Jesus: The Model of Victory-Centered Warfare

Jesus never waged warfare from desperation. He spoke with authority, withdrew strategically, and remained aligned with the Father's will. Even when opposition intensified, He did not rush or strive. His confidence was rooted in relationship and assignment.

At the cross, what appeared to be ultimate defeat, Jesus declared completion.

John 19:30 (NKJV)
"It is finished."

That declaration was not resignation; it was victory. The war was settled. Every act of intercession now flows from that finished work.

Victory is not the reward of warfare.
Victory is the foundation of warfare.

When intercessors pray from this truth, strongholds are confronted without fear, endurance replaces exhaustion, and obedience is sustained without collapse. The enemy is not being chased, he is being reminded of what has already been decided.

Declarations

- I declare that Christ has already secured victory over every opposing power.

- I fight from victory, not toward it.

- I put on the full armor of God and engage warfare with clarity and confidence.

- I wield the Word of God as my primary weapon.

- I stand firm, unmoved by delay, resistance, or intimidation.

- I declare that I stand firm in the finished work of Christ and refuse to be moved by fear, delay, or resistance

- I declare that opposition does not dictate my posture; God's Word does. I remain unmoved and unshaken.

Prayer

Lord, reposition my heart and my posture.
Teach me to pray from rest, not striving.
Help me to stand firm in Your victory
and to wield Your Word with wisdom and authority.
I receive my position in Christ.
Give me the grace to stand firm in faith, trusting Your finished work
even when nothing around me seems to move.

In Jesus' Name Amen.

Reader Reflection

(Journal or meditate prayerfully)

1. Have I been praying as though victory depended on my effort rather than Christ's finished work?

2. Which piece of the armor do I tend to neglect during prolonged warfare?

3. Where has striving replaced standing in my prayer life?

4. How does knowing the battle is already decided change how I pray today?

5. Where am I feeling pressure to do more, when God is actually inviting me to stand, trust, and hold the ground He has already given me?

Word of Encouragement

I want to pause right here and give a word of encouragement to the Gods Prayer Warriors and Intercessors.

If you are reading this, I believe the Lord has already been drawing you closer not with urgency, but with intention. You are here because your heart has learned to listen, and because God has entrusted you with a sensitivity that is precious to Him. This calling you carry is sacred, even when it feels heavy.

I know there have been moments when you wondered if your prayers were heard, when answers felt slow, or when the weight of standing for others felt lonely. I want to gently remind you of this truth: none of your prayers have been wasted. Every whispered intercession, every silent stand, every act of obedience offered in faith has been seen by Heaven.

You were never asked to carry this perfectly.
You were simply invited to carry it faithfully.

If pressure has crept in, pressure to pray more, do more, or get it right, I encourage you to lay that down. Precision in prayer is not something you force; it is something the Holy Spirit forms in you as you walk with Him. God is not measuring your effectiveness by effort, but by alignment. He is far more interested in your nearness than your noise.

You do not have to pray everything you see.
You do not have to carry every burden you feel.
You are only asked to steward what God places in your hands.

As you learn to listen, your prayers will become quieter but stronger. More focused. More restful. And more fruitful.

If you are tired, you are not weak.
If you are still learning, you are not late.
If you are standing, you are being sustained by grace.

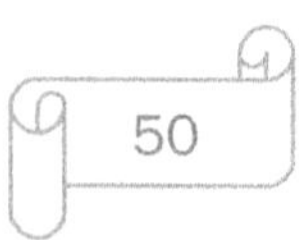

Remember this: you are praying from victory, not striving toward it. You are standing in authority, not reaching for approval. God Himself surrounds you; He is your covering, your guide, and your reward.

So, continue, gently.
Stay yielded.
Stay listening.

You are seen.
You are held.
You are equipped for this season.

With deep honor for your calling,
Your fellow Intercessor,

Sabrina

Chapter 4: Praying With Precision
Apostolic Intercession

Once position is established, precision becomes essential. Authority without accuracy can lead to misdirected effort, unnecessary fatigue, and ineffective prayer. But when intercession flows from victory and is governed by discernment, prayer becomes focused, intentional, and powerful.

Praying with precision does not mean praying perfectly, it means praying aligned. Apostolic intercession is not driven by emotion, urgency, or visible pressure; it is shaped by Heaven's perspective. Precision begins when the intercessor understands that prayer is not about informing God of a problem, but partnering with Him to enforce His will.

Jesus modeled this kind of prayer consistently. He did not pray reactively; He prayed relationally and obediently. His prayers flowed from intimacy with the Father and alignment with divine purpose.

John 5:19 (NKJV)
"The Son can do nothing of Himself, but what He sees the Father do…"

This statement reveals the foundation of accurate prayer: seeing before speaking. Apostolic intercession begins with listening. The intercessor learns to discern what God is doing, where He is moving, and what He is addressing, then joins Him there.

What Is Apostolic Intercession?

Apostolic intercession is prayer that flows from being sent. It is not merely devotional prayer, crisis prayer, or personal petition; it is intercession aligned with Heaven's assignment to establish, protect, and advance the purposes of God in the earth. The word

apostolic comes from the Greek *apostolos*, meaning *one who is sent with authority*. Apostolic intercession, therefore, is prayer offered from a place of authorization rather than emotion.

This form of intercession does not pray aimlessly or reactively. It prays according to divine instruction, timing, and purpose. Apostolic intercessors stand in the gap not only to request God's intervention, but to enforce what God has already decreed. Their prayers are grounded in Scripture, guided by the Holy Spirit, and focused on assignment rather than circumstance.

John 20:21 (NKJV)
"As the Father has sent Me, I also send you."

Apostolic intercession carries the weight of responsibility. It recognizes that not every burden is assigned, and not every battle is to be engaged. Instead, the intercessor discerns what God is addressing in a given season and joins Him there. This type of prayer often targets foundations, strongholds, systems, mindsets, and spiritual resistance that oppose God's will, rather than surface-level symptoms.

2 Corinthians 10:3–5 (NKJV)
"For the weapons of our warfare are not carnal but mighty in God for pulling down strongholds..."

Apostolic intercession also includes endurance. Because it is assignment-based, it often requires sustained prayer over time rather than immediate breakthrough. The intercessor remains faithful not because outcomes are visible, but because obedience is required.

Colossians 4:12 (NKJV)
"...always laboring fervently for you in prayers..."

At its core, apostolic intercession is partnership. It is Heaven inviting human obedience into divine purpose. The intercessor does not replace God's authority but operates under it, praying

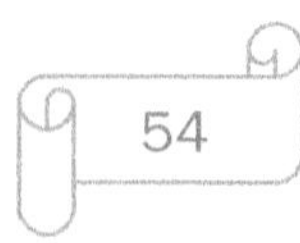

from victory, aligned with Christ's finished work, and led by the Spirit.

Apostolic Intercession Modeled in the Prayers of the Apostles

Apostolic intercession does not originate from modern terminology or spiritual trends, it is drawn directly from the prayer life of the apostles in the New Testament. The apostles did not pray generically or emotionally; they prayed with clarity, authority, and purpose, aligned with God's redemptive plan for the Church. Their prayers reveal how intercession functions when one is sent with divine authority.

When we examine apostolic prayers, especially those of Paul, we notice a distinct pattern: they are root-focused rather than symptom-focused, kingdom-centered rather than circumstance-driven, and transformational rather than transactional. These prayers were not primarily about changing situations, but about establishing spiritual strength, revelation, maturity, and authority in believers.

For example, Paul's prayer in Ephesians does not ask for relief from persecution or easier circumstances. Instead, it targets spiritual illumination and authority.

Ephesians 1:17–19 (NKJV)
"...that the God of our Lord Jesus Christ... may give to you the spirit of wisdom and revelation in the knowledge of Him, the eyes of your understanding being enlightened..."

This is apostolic intercession at work, praying for revelation because revelation changes everything. Paul understood that when believers see correctly, they live correctly. Precision in prayer begins by addressing spiritual perception.

Similarly, Paul's prayer in Colossians focuses on alignment, endurance, and fruitfulness rather than immediate deliverance.

Colossians 1:9–11 (NKJV)

"...that you may be filled with the knowledge of His will in all wisdom and spiritual understanding; that you may walk worthy of the Lord..."

This prayer reflects apostolic precision. Paul intercedes for internal transformation that would sustain believers through external opposition. He understood that lasting victory flows from spiritual maturity, not circumstantial ease.

Even Paul's warfare prayers reflect discipline and accuracy. He did not pray aimlessly, nor did he engage opposition without clarity.

Apostolic intercession, therefore, draws its framework from these prayers. It teaches intercessors how to pray with intent, authority, and alignment, addressing foundations rather than surface issues, and partnering with God's long-term purposes rather than short-term relief.

When intercessors pray apostolically, they are praying in continuity with the New Testament pattern. They are joining the same stream of Spirit-led, assignment-focused prayer that established churches, strengthened believers, and advanced the Kingdom in the face of sustained resistance.

If precision feels unfamiliar or intimidating, remember this: God does not expect you to master accuracy overnight. Precision develops through obedience, intimacy, and practice. The Holy Spirit is your guide, and He leads gently.

John 16:13 (NKJV)

"However, when He, the Spirit of truth, has come, He will guide you into all truth..."

You are not required to pray everything—only what God assigns. Accuracy grows as trust deepens.

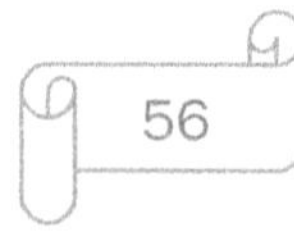

Accuracy Begins with Discernment

Precision in prayer requires discernment. Not every problem is the same, and not every battle requires the same response. Without discernment, prayer becomes scattered, addressing symptoms rather than roots, reacting to noise rather than responding to truth.

Scripture teaches that discernment is developed through maturity and practice.

Hebrews 5:14 (NKJV)
"But solid food belongs to those who are of full age... who by reason of use have their senses exercised to discern both good and evil."

Apostolic intercession trains the intercessor to ask different questions:

- What is Heaven highlighting in this moment?

- Is this resistance to confront, endure, or ignore?

- What has God already spoken concerning this matter?

Accuracy increases when the intercessor refuses to pray from assumption and instead prays from revelation.

The Word as the Measure of Precision

The Word of God is the standard by which all accurate prayer is measured. Precision is impossible without Scripture. Emotional prayer may express concern, but Word-based prayer executes authority.

Hebrews 4:12 (NKJV)
"For the word of God is living and powerful, and sharper than any two-edged sword..."

The Word cuts through confusion, exposes deception, and confronts strongholds directly. Apostolic intercession is not built on opinion, or urgency is built on declaration. The intercessor does not argue with darkness; they confront it with truth.

When prayer is saturated with Scripture:

- Faith is strengthened

- Discernment is sharpened

- Authority is enforced

The Word ensures that prayer remains aligned with Heaven rather than shaped by circumstances.

Praying What God Has Already Spoken

Accuracy in prayer increases when the intercessor learns to pray what God has already declared. God's promises reveal His intentions, and intercession enforces those intentions on earth.

Isaiah 55:11 (NKJV)
*"So shall My word be that goes forth from My mouth;
It shall not return to Me void..."*

Apostolic intercession agrees with God's Word even when visible reality contradicts it. Precision is choosing agreement over observation. The intercessor does not deny circumstances but refuses to let them define prayer.

This is how prayer remains effective without becoming exhausting. The intercessor is not trying to convince God to act, they are aligning with what He has already said He will do.

Restraint: Knowing When Not to Pray

Precision also requires restraint. Not every situation requires immediate vocal prayer. Sometimes accuracy means standing silently, waiting, or allowing God to work without interference. Jesus often withdrew, not because He lacked power, but because He honored timing.

Luke 5:16 (NKJV)

"So He Himself often withdrew into the wilderness and prayed."

Restraint protects the intercessor from burnout and misdirected warfare. Accurate prayer understands that silence, waiting, and standing are sometimes the most powerful responses.

Apostolic Intercession Is Assignment-Focused

Apostolic prayer is not scattered across every need, it is focused on assignment. Precision sharpens when the intercessor understands what God has entrusted to them to carry.

Paul demonstrates this clarity when he speaks of purposeful engagement.

1 Corinthians 9:26 (NKJV)
"Therefore I run thus: not with uncertainty. Thus I fight: not as one who beats the air."

Intercessors called to apostolic prayer learn to pray with intention, clarity, and discipline. They know their lane. They know their assignment. And they remain faithful within it.

Declarations

- I declare that I am sent by God and authorized to pray according to His will.
- I pray with precision, discernment, and alignment—not emotion or urgency.
- I engage only the battles Heaven has assigned to me.
- My prayers target roots, not symptoms.
- I do not fight aimlessly; I enforce Heaven's agenda with clarity and restraint.
- I win through strategic prayers that are grounded in truth and guided by the Spirit.

Prayer

Holy Spirit, thank You for training my discernment and steadying my posture. Teach me to recognize when resistance is not a sign to retreat, but a call to stand. Guard me from confusion and from

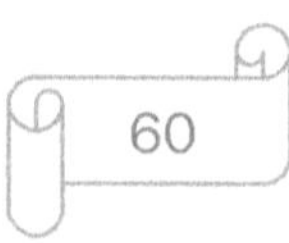

striving.
Help me to remain aligned as You reveal what must be addressed next. I trust Your timing, Your strategy, and Your authority at work through me. Amen.

Reader Reflection

(Journal or meditate prayerfully)

1. Where has prayer become clearer, yet resistance remains?

2. Am I interpreting resistance as failure, or as revelation?

3. What patterns, pressures, or obstacles have persisted despite alignment?

4. Is God inviting me to move from precision into confrontation?

Chapter 5: Confronting Strongholds
Dismantling What Resists God's Will

This chapter marks a shift.

Until now, the work of the intercessor has centered on alignment, learning to pray accurately, to listen before speaking, and to stand from victory rather than striving for it. But there comes a point in warfare when precision alone is no longer sufficient. Accurate prayer does not always remove resistance; often, it exposes it.

Scripture is honest about this reality. Some opposition is not momentary or circumstantial but entrenched. It has learned how to remain. It has adapted to seasons of prayer, survived moments of alignment, and endured long enough to become fortified. This is where the language of Scripture changes. What was once described as opposition is now revealed as a stronghold.

Strongholds represent resistance that has settled in. They are not merely problems to be solved or struggles to be endured; they are positions that actively resist the will of God. Awareness may identify them. Prayer may illuminate them. Alignment may clarify them. But there are moments when none of these, by themselves, are enough to remove what has been allowed to stand for so long.

This is where confrontation becomes necessary, not emotional confrontation, not reactive engagement, but intentional, authorized, and obedient confrontation. Scripture never treats confrontation as reckless or aggressive. It presents it as measured, purposeful, and governed by divine instruction. To confront is not to abandon prayer; it is to apply authority where resistance has been revealed.

Biblical Strongholds: Personal and Systemic

Scripture reveals that strongholds are not uniform in form. They appear both within individuals and beyond them, embedded in systems, cultures, and regions. Understanding this distinction is critical, because the way a stronghold is confronted must align with the nature of its resistance.

Some strongholds are deeply personal, rooted in the inner life. They take shape in the mind, emotions, and will, often beginning as vulnerabilities that go unaddressed. Saul's life illustrates this form of resistance. Though chosen and anointed by God (1 Samuel 10:1), Saul allowed insecurity and fear to remain unresolved. Over time, these internal fractures hardened into fortified opposition.

His jealousy toward David was not merely relational conflict; it was resistance to God's unfolding purpose. Scripture records that *"an evil spirit from the Lord troubled him"* as Saul continued to resist alignment **(1 Samuel 16:14, NKJV)**. What began as insecurity matured into hostility, and what was tolerated internally eventually opposed God's will externally.

Saul's story reveals a sobering truth: anointing does not dismantle strongholds. Authority does not remove resistance when surrender is withheld. Personal strongholds persist when inner opposition is allowed to coexist with outward obedience. The resistance remains not because God is silent, but because the heart refuses alignment.

Other strongholds are systemic, operating beyond the individual and sustained by collective agreement, power, and structure. Egypt stands as one of Scripture's clearest examples. Pharaoh's resistance was not merely personal stubbornness; it represented an entire system built on oppression, fear, and control. Israel's bondage was maintained not by ignorance, but by an entrenched order that resisted God's promise (Exodus 1–12).

Deliverance did not occur when the problem was recognized. It required confrontation, repeated, obedient, and sustained, until the system itself was dismantled. Each plague confronted not only Pharaoh's will but the spiritual and structural foundations of Egypt's power. Liberation came only when resistance was fully confronted and broken.

Jericho offers another picture of systemic strongholds. Its walls symbolized more than military defense; they represented long-standing resistance to God's promise (Joshua 6). The city had learned how to stand. It had endured previous threats and fortified itself against invasion. Yet Jericho did not fall because Israel acknowledged the walls. It fell because Israel obeyed God's instruction precisely and persistently. The stronghold collapsed when divine authority met obedient endurance.

These examples reveal that strongholds, whether personal or systemic, are sustained by longevity rather than intensity. They remain because they have learned how to endure unchallenged. What defines a stronghold is not how loudly it resists, but how long it has remained.

Why Some Strongholds Persist

Strongholds often persist because they are misunderstood. Many assume that continued resistance indicates ineffective prayer or spiritual failure. Scripture, however, presents a different picture. Persistent resistance often signals depth. What is deeply rooted requires more than momentary engagement; it demands intentional, sustained confrontation governed by wisdom and timing.

Some strongholds remain because they have been prayed *around* rather than addressed *directly*. Prayer brings awareness, alignment, and clarity, but confrontation addresses authority. Until authority is exercised at the point where resistance is fortified, the stronghold remains intact. This does not diminish the value of prayer; it clarifies its progression. Prayer reveals. Confrontation dismantles.

Others persist because timing has not yet aligned. Scripture repeatedly shows that God delays engagement not out of reluctance, but out of preparation. Israel wandered before inheriting (Deuteronomy 8). David fled before reigning (1 Samuel 19–31). Even Jesus did not confront every system simultaneously, declaring that He did only what He saw the Father doing (John 5:19). Delay does not mean denial. Often, it means alignment is still forming, within the intercessor as much as within the moment.

Strongholds also persist when engagement exceeds assignment. Discernment may reveal many things, but authority operates only within the boundaries God establishes. When intercessors confront resistance, they have not been authorized to engage, opposition hardens rather than yields. Effort multiplies, but impact diminishes. Scripture consistently demonstrates that victory flows from obedience, not enthusiasm. This is why confrontation must never be separated from wisdom, and why the intercessor, once awakened to resistance, must also learn how to remain steady without burning out.

Finally, some strongholds remain because dismantling them requires endurance rather than intensity. Scripture emphasizes persistence more than spectacle. Walls fall after circling. Deliverance follows obedience over time. Dominion is established through faithfulness, not force. Strongholds that have endured for years are rarely removed in moments; they are outlasted.

Strongholds do not fall by awareness alone. They are dismantled through obedient confrontation, sustained alignment, and divine timing. Precision exposes them. Authority engages them. Endurance outlasts them.

Here is an example of a regional stronghold:

Poverty Normalized as Identity

In some regions, poverty becomes more than an economic condition, it becomes an accepted identity. Generations grow up believing limitation is inevitable, advancement is unrealistic, and abundance is for others. This mindset is reinforced by systems, policies, and repeated disappointment, creating a fortified resistance to hope.

Prayer may bring awareness and compassion, but awareness alone does not break the stronghold. The resistance persists because the system has learned how to endure. Dismantling it requires sustained, strategic engagement, intercession paired with obedience, wisdom, and long-term faithfulness. Endurance outlasts resignation. As alignment shifts and truth is established, the stronghold weakens, making room for generational change.

Personal stronghold:

A common example of a personal stronghold is generational fear that manifests as chronic hesitation and self-protection. A person may be faithful, prayerful, and sincere, yet consistently retreat from obedience when risk is involved. Opportunities arise, leadership, speaking, advancement, or influence—but are repeatedly deferred. On the surface, this appears as caution or humility. In reality, fear has been allowed to remain unchallenged long enough to become fortified.

Awareness alone does not dismantle this kind of resistance. The individual may recognize the pattern, pray for peace, and even confess Scripture, yet still find themselves unable to move forward. The stronghold persists because fear is not merely an emotion; it has become a governing voice. It shapes decisions, limits obedience, and resists God's unfolding purpose.

Dismantling this stronghold requires obedient confrontation. At some point, alignment must move beyond agreement into action. Authority is exercised when the person obeys despite fear—

speaking when silence feels safer, stepping forward when retreat feels justified. Endurance becomes necessary because the resistance does not disappear immediately. Fear protests when it loses control. But over time, consistent obedience weakens its structure until it no longer governs.

What was once a stronghold becomes a testimony, not because fear was absent, but because authority was sustained long enough to outlast it.

What Is Obedient Confrontation?

Obedient confrontation is the deliberate choice to act in alignment with God's instruction at the precise point where resistance has been exposed. It is not emotional defiance, self-generated courage, or aggressive striving. It is obedience expressed through action, sustained over time, in the face of opposition.

In the context of a stronghold like generational fear, obedient confrontation does not begin by trying to "feel fearless." It begins by obeying while fear is still present, in other words do it scared.

What It Means to Dismantle

To dismantle is not merely to disrupt or weaken; it is to take apart deliberately and completely. In Scripture, dismantling speaks to the removal of structure, not just pressure. A dismantled stronghold is one that can no longer support itself, defend its position, or reassert its influence.

Dismantling differs from momentary breakthrough. Breakthrough creates access; dismantling removes infrastructure. When a stronghold is dismantled, its power source is cut off, its authority is revoked, and its ability to resist is undone. This work is often slower than expected, not because God hesitates, but because dismantling addresses foundations rather than appearances.

Biblically, dismantling involves sustained obedience, correct authority, and divine timing. Walls do not fall until circling is

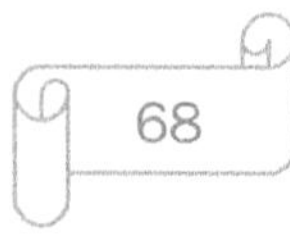

complete. Systems do not collapse until confrontation is thorough. Inner resistance does not dissolve until surrender is full. To dismantle is to remain present until what once stood no longer has permission or power to remain.

This is why dismantling requires endurance. Strongholds are not impressed by intensity; they yield to persistence governed by obedience. The intercessor does not rush dismantling, nor do they abandon it prematurely. They stay aligned, steady, and submitted trusting that what God has authorized to be dismantled will not survive sustained truth and authority.

This is the moment when prayer shifts in posture. The intercessor realizes, quietly but unmistakably:

I am not just praying, I am now responsible to confront and dismantle.

And with that realization comes the need for steadiness, restraint, and endurance—lessons that must be learned if the fire of warfare is to be sustained without consuming the one who carries it.

Prayer

Lord, grant me the wisdom to discern what must be confronted and the endurance to remain present until Your work is complete. Keep my heart aligned, my spirit steady, and my obedience intact. I trust Your timing, Your authority, and Your purpose at work through me.   In Jesus' Name, Amen.

Declarations

- I declare that discernment reveals what must be dismantled.

- I declare that I do not confront resistance prematurely or avoid it fearfully.

- I declare that what God has authorized me to confront will not withstand His truth.

- I declare that I dismantle strongholds through obedience, endurance, and alignment.

- I declare that resistance loses its structure, its influence, and its right to remain.

- I declare that I remain steady until what stands against God's will is fully undone.

Reader Reflection

(Journal or meditate prayerfully)

1. What resistance has remained despite clarity, prayer, and alignment?

2. Am I seeking quick relief, or am I willing to remain present until dismantling is complete?

3. Have I confused disruption with dismantling in my own expectations?

4. What might God be inviting me to outlast rather than overcome quickly?

Dear Intercessor

A Quiet Commissioning

This is not a commissioning marked by public recognition or dramatic declaration.
It is quieter than that and weightier.

To see resistance clearly is to be entrusted with responsibility.
To recognize a stronghold is to be invited into obedience, not reaction.

From this point forward, the intercessor does not engage blindly or emotionally. They move with clarity, restraint, and resolve.

This is the moment when awareness becomes assignment.
When discernment gives way to obedience.
When the intercessor understands that authority must be stewarded, not displayed.

Nothing needs to be announced.
Nothing needs to be proven.
The work will speak for itself.

Please know that confrontation is not a moment—it is a process.
And processes require endurance.

- Once strongholds are exposed and engagement begins, the greater challenge emerges:
- how to remain steady when resistance does not lift quickly,
- how to sustain obedience when intensity fades, and
- how to guard the heart when warfare becomes prolonged.

This next chapter turns our attention to that necessity.
Because dismantling resistance is not only about authority—it is about longevity.   That is where we now turn.

Chapter 6: Sustaining the Fire

Confrontation is not the end of warfare; it is the beginning of endurance.

When strongholds are exposed and engagement begins, the nature of the battle changes. What once required clarity now requires consistency. What once demanded courage now demands faithfulness. The intercessor quickly learns that dismantling resistance is rarely dramatic or swift. It is steady. It is prolonged. And it requires a different kind of strength.

Many intercessors are prepared for intensity but unprepared for longevity. They know how to press in moments of urgency but sustaining obedience when resistance does not immediately lift can feel disorienting. This is where many grow weary, not because the assignment is unclear, but because the fire must now be maintained rather than ignited.

Scripture speaks often of fire, but it rarely presents it as fleeting. The fire God entrusts is meant to remain. It must be tended, guarded, and sustained. Without care, even holy fire can consume the one who carries it. Without rhythm, even righteous passion can lead to exhaustion.

Sustaining the fire does not mean striving harder or praying louder. It means learning how to remain faithful without burning out, how to stay obedient without becoming rigid, and how to carry authority without letting warfare define identity. This chapter is not about increasing intensity; it is about preserving integrity.

God never intended the intercessor to live in a constant state of urgency. Warfare that lasts requires rest that is intentional. Authority that endures requires humility that remains. Fire that continues to burn must be supplied by obedience, not adrenaline.

This is where wisdom becomes essential. Not every season of warfare is marked by visible progress. Not every confrontation produces immediate breakthrough. Yet Scripture makes clear that sustained obedience carries weight even when results are unseen. What is being built in the intercessor during prolonged warfare is as important as what is being dismantled in the spirit.

Sustaining the fire is about learning how to stand when there is no movement, how to pray when answers are delayed, and how to remain aligned when the battle feels quiet but unresolved. It is the discipline of remaining present without becoming consumed.

If Chapter 5 awakened responsibility, this chapter teaches stewardship.

Because the fire entrusted to the intercessor is not meant to burn them, it is meant to remain.

Weariness does not always come from disobedience. Often, it comes from faithfulness stretched over time.

Many intercessors burn out not because they lack passion, but because they attempt to carry prolonged warfare with short-term rhythms. They remain alert, vigilant, and engaged long after the initial urgency has passed, without adjusting how they carry the assignment. Over time, what began as devotion becomes depletion—not because the fire was wrong, but because it was not being sustained properly.

Scripture does not shame weariness; it addresses it. God never rebukes His servants for needing rest. Instead, He provides instruction for how fire is meant to remain without consuming the one who tends it, (Isaiah 43:2). Holy fire was never intended to be chaotic or self-generated. It was meant to be stewarded.

Isaiah 43:2 (NKJV)
"When you walk through the fire, you shall not be burned, nor shall the flame scorch you."

There was a season in my own life when weariness settled in quietly.

I was not rebelling. I was not disengaged. I was still praying, still listening, still standing. Yet beneath the surface, exhaustion began to erode clarity. The weight was not dramatic, it was steady. Day after day of obedience without visible movement. Prayer without immediate relief. Responsibility without rest.

It was there that I learned how subtly the enemy works with fatigue.

He did not tempt me to sin. He tempted me to stop.
He did not question my calling. He questioned my endurance.
He did not attack my faith outright. He whispered that faithfulness was costing too much.

Weariness became the opening. Not because I lacked devotion, but because prolonged faithfulness had gone unguarded. In that place, the enemy did not roar, he suggested. He framed restlessness as wisdom, withdrawal as protection, silence as relief. And slowly, the temptation was not to abandon prayer altogether, but to disengage just enough to lose ground.

This is how many intercessors quit, not through failure, but through fatigue.

The enemy understands that an intercessor who remains steady is dangerous. When confrontation does not stop them, exhaustion is often deployed instead. If he cannot steal authority, he attempts to drain stamina. If he cannot silence prayer through fear, he attempts to wear it down through delay.

That season forced me to confront a truth I had overlooked: sustaining the fire requires guarding the vessel. I had learned how to contend, but I had not yet learned how to pace obedience. I had honored the assignment, but I had neglected the rhythm that would allow me to carry it long-term.

God did not remove the assignment in that season. He refined the posture. He did not release me from responsibility; He taught me how to remain without burning out. The restoration did not come through increased intensity, but through realignment, learning when to withdraw, when to rest, and when to let obedience remain simple.

That season taught me this: the enemy does not need to defeat an intercessor if he can exhaust one.

This is why sustaining the fire is not optional. It is a safeguard. Without it, even those called to endure may quietly step back, not because they were unfaithful, but because they were tired.

The priesthood offers one of Scripture's clearest pictures of sustained fire. In the tabernacle, the fire on the altar was commanded to remain burning continually (Leviticus 6:12–13). Yet the priests were not told to create the fire repeatedly. They were instructed to tend it, adding wood daily, removing ashes, and maintaining order. The work was routine, deliberate, and uncelebrated. Sustaining the fire required rhythm, not intensity.

Leviticus 6:12–13 (NKJV)
"And the fire on the altar shall be kept burning on it; it shall not be put out... A fire shall always be burning on the altar; it shall never go out."

This pattern reveals a vital truth: holy fire is preserved through consistency, not crisis. When intercessors attempt to live perpetually at the altar without rhythm, rest, or renewal, even sacred work becomes exhausting. But when obedience is paired with structure, the fire remains without consuming the priest.

The watchmen of Scripture reflect this same endurance. Positioned on the walls, they were responsible for remaining alert through long stretches of quiet. Their role was not constant action, but faithful presence. Scripture describes watchmen who "never hold their peace day or night" (Isaiah 62:6), not because they were frantic, but because they were assigned to remain. Their strength was not measured by visible victories, but by their ability to stay.

Isaiah 62:6 (NKJV)
"I have set watchmen on your walls, O Jerusalem;
They shall never hold their peace day or night.
You who make mention of the Lord, do not keep silent."

Watchmen understood that silence did not mean inactivity and stillness did not signal retreat. Their authority lay in consistency. They stayed when others slept. They remained when nothing seemed to change. Sustaining the fire for them meant resisting discouragement during seasons when obedience felt repetitive and results were unseen.

The apostle Paul embodies this endurance on a personal level. His letters reveal a man acquainted with prolonged resistance, pressure without release, opposition without immediate resolution. Yet Paul did not burn out; he adjusted his posture. He learned to pace obedience, to rejoice without relief, and to remain faithful without applause. His endurance flowed not from relentless effort, but from alignment with grace. As he wrote, *"I labor, striving according to His working which works in me mightily"* **(Colossians 1:29, NKJV)**.

Paul's life reminds the intercessor that sustained fire is not fueled by self-effort. It is sustained by partnership with God's strength. Burnout occurs when responsibility is carried alone. Endurance emerges when obedience remains tethered to grace.

Holy rhythm, then, is not a luxury, it is a safeguard. It teaches the intercessor when to engage and when to withdraw, when to speak and when to stand silently, when to labor and when to rest. Rhythm honors both the assignment and the vessel carrying it.

Let me explain what Holy rhythm is:

Holy rhythm is the grace of God governing the pace of warfare so that fire remains without consuming the one who tends it.

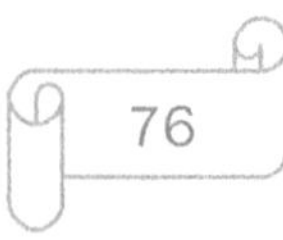

Holy rhythm is the God-established pace by which an intercessor remains effective without being consumed. It is the ordered flow of prayer, obedience, rest, and restraint that allows spiritual fire to remain burning without exhausting the vessel tending it.

Holy rhythm recognizes that warfare is not a sprint but a sustained assignment. Unlike urgency—which demands constant output, holy rhythm is governed by obedience to timing. It allows the intercessor to engage when instructed, withdraw when led, and remain steady across seasons rather than reactive in moments.

In Scripture, holy rhythm is never passive. It is intentional alignment with God's pace. Fire remains on the altar, but it is tended according to divine order, not human strain.

What Holy Rhythm Is *Not*

Holy rhythm is not:

- Inconsistency

- Withdrawal from assignment

- Laziness or disengagement

- Ignoring burden

- Loss of intensity

Instead, it is disciplined sustainability.

Sustaining the fire requires humility, the humility to acknowledge limits, to obey without urgency, and to trust that God is at work even when progress feels slow. It is the discipline of remaining faithful without becoming frantic, committed without becoming consumed.

This chapter does not ask the intercessor to do more. It invites them to remain wise.

Because the fire entrusted to you is not meant to burn you out. It is meant to burn steadily, long enough to finish the work.

Scripture never portrays obedience as chaotic or unbounded. Even the most intense seasons of warfare are framed by moments of withdrawal, silence, and restraint. Jesus Himself modeled this rhythm. Though surrounded by need and opposition, He often withdrew, not to disengage from assignment, but to remain aligned within it. His obedience was unwavering, yet His pace was governed.

Rest, in this sense, is not retreat. It is recalibration. It is the act of returning the weight of responsibility back to God so that obedience remains light enough to carry. When rest is neglected, the intercessor begins to carry outcomes instead of assignment. Weariness follows not because the work is wrong, but because the burden has shifted.

Obedience, too, must remain simple. Sustained warfare tempts the intercessor to overcomplicate faithfulness, to add effort where God has not added instruction. Scripture consistently honors obedience that is clear and uncomplicated. The fire remains when the intercessor does what God has asked, no more and no less. Longevity is preserved when obedience is not embellished.

Boundaries function quietly but powerfully in this process. Boundaries are not barriers to ministry; they are protections for it. They define where responsibility ends and trust begins. Without boundaries, the intercessor absorbs what was never assigned to carry. Over time, this erodes clarity, drains strength, and dulls discernment.

Again, holy rhythm teaches the intercessor how to remain engaged without being consumed. It allows the fire to burn steadily rather than violently. It makes space for recovery without guilt and for restraint without fear. Sustaining the fire is not about proving endurance, it is about preserving obedience.

As warfare continues, the intercessor learns that staying requires as much wisdom as advancing. Not every moment calls for confrontation. Not every silence signal defeat. Often, the most faithful act is simply remaining aligned present, watchful, and at rest in God's authority.

This is how the fire lasts.

Prayer

Lord, You see the fire You have entrusted to me. Teach me how to tend it without striving and carry it without being consumed.
Where weariness has settled in, restore strength that comes from alignment, not effort.
Help me remain faithful in prolonged seasons and steady when progress feels slow.
Guard my heart from urgency that produces exhaustion
and anchor my obedience in Your grace and timing.
Let Your strength work in me mightily as I labor according to Your will. I commit to remain—watchful, obedient, and sustained by You.

In Jesus' Name Amen.

Declaration

- I declare that my obedience will outlast weariness.

- I declare that fatigue will not silence my calling or erode my resolve.

- I release every burden I was never assigned to carry.

- I receive strength that comes from alignment, not effort.

- I choose rhythm over urgency and faithfulness over intensity.

- I remain engaged without being consumed and committed without burning out.

- The fire entrusted to me will burn steadily—long enough to finish the work.

Reader Reflection

(Journal or meditate prayerfully)

Not to evaluate your faithfulness, but to notice your pace.

There are seasons when obedience is steady yet heavy, when prayer continues but strength quietly thins. Sometimes weariness does not announce itself as discouragement; it appears as dullness, hesitation, or the subtle temptation to step back just enough to feel relief.

Ask yourself gently:

1. Where has prolonged faithfulness begun to cost more than I expected?

2. Have I mistaken exhaustion for wisdom, or withdrawal for protection?

3. Am I carrying responsibility God never asked me to manage alone?

4. What rhythm might the Spirit be inviting me to recover, not to escape the work, but to remain in it?

These questions are not meant to accuse.
They are meant to preserve.

Many intercessors do not abandon their assignment; they simply grow tired inside it. And fatigue, when left unattended, can quietly erode clarity, resolve, and joy. This reflection is an invitation to tend what God has entrusted to you, including your own strength.

Let the Lord meet you here, not to remove your calling, but to sustain it. Amen!

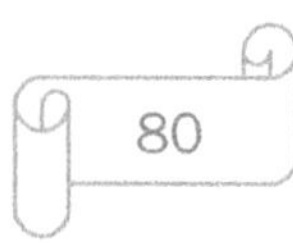

Chapter 7: Friendly Fire

Biblical Definition of Friendly Fire

In warfare, friendly fire refers to harm inflicted unintentionally by one's own side. Spiritually, the concept is similar. Friendly fire occurs when damage comes not from the enemy's direct assault, but from misalignment, immaturity, or unguarded posture within covenant relationships.

Scripture does not use the modern term, but it describes the reality plainly. Friendly fire is not betrayal; it is breakdown. It emerges when those assigned to stand together lose alignment in heart, posture, or discernment. The intent is not always malicious, but the impact is real.

Biblically, friendly fire happens when spiritual authority is exercised without humility, when correction is offered without gentleness, or when pressure exposes unresolved issues within the soul. It wounds not because truth is absent, but because love, timing, or restraint is missing.

Friendly fire is especially dangerous because it comes from familiar voices. The words carry weight. Proximity creates trust. And when alignment fractures, the damage often goes unrecognized until strength has already been drained.

Scripture treats this kind of internal harm seriously—not to assign blame, but to preserve the people God has called to endure.

Biblical Examples of Friendly Fire

Moses, Miriam, and Aaron (Numbers 12)

One of Scripture's clearest examples of friendly fire appears within leadership itself.

Miriam and Aaron spoke against Moses, not as outsiders, but as siblings and co-laborers in God's work. Their words were framed as concern, yet Scripture exposes the root as jealousy and misalignment. What should have been protected through honor was exposed through complaint.

God's response was decisive. He did not ignore the damage because of relationship. He intervened to preserve order, authority, and alignment. This account reveals that friendly fire often begins when familiarity replaces reverence and calling is questioned rather than covered.

David and Saul's House (1 Samuel 18–20, NKJV)

David's greatest wounds did not come from Philistine battlefields, but from within Israel's leadership.

Saul's insecurity turned inward pressure into outward hostility. Jonathan was torn between loyalty to his father and covenant with David. Michal's love became entangled with fear. David found himself navigating suspicion, manipulation, and misunderstanding—not from enemies, but from those closest to the throne.

This was friendly fire fueled by insecurity and unprocessed fear. David did not retaliate. He withdrew, when necessary, remained aligned, and entrusted vindication to God. His restraint preserved both his calling and his heart.

The Disciples Among Themselves (Luke 22:24, NKJV)

Even those closest to Jesus were not immune to internal erosion.

Scripture records that *"there was also a dispute among them, as to which of them should be considered the greatest."* This occurred not in ignorance, but on the eve of the cross. Pressure revealed ambition. Proximity did not prevent comparison.

Jesus did not rebuke their calling; He corrected their posture. He reframed leadership as servanthood and authority as humility.

This moment shows that friendly fire can emerge even in holy proximity when formation lags behind responsibility.

The Early Church (Galatians 5:15, NKJV)

Paul addresses friendly fire directly when he warns the church, *"But if you bite and devour one another, beware lest you be consumed by one another."*

The danger was not persecution; it was internal fracture. Paul understood that a community under pressure could turn inward if love and restraint were not maintained. The threat was not doctrinal collapse, but relational erosion.

This warning reveals that friendly fire does not require false teaching to be destructive. Unchecked words, wounded pride, and unresolved offense are sufficient.

Why These Examples Matter

These accounts reveal a consistent pattern: friendly fire emerges most often among the called, not the careless.

It arises in environments of pressure, proximity, and responsibility. It does not negate calling, but it does test maturity. Scripture includes these stories not to shame, but to instruct, so that those called to endure do not destroy one another in the process.

Discerning Friendly Fire Without Becoming Defensive

Recognizing friendly fire requires discernment without suspicion.

Scripture reminds us that not every wound is an attack, and not every discomfort is damage. *"Faithful are the wounds of a friend, but the kisses of an enemy are deceitful"* **(Proverbs 27:6, NKJV)**. There are moments when correction sharpens, strengthens, and realigns. Yet there are also moments when words spoken without humility or timing cease to refine and instead erode.

Jesus Himself modeled this discernment. Though surrounded by followers, Scripture records that *"Jesus did not commit Himself to*

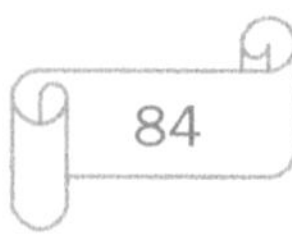

them, because He knew all men" **(John 2:24, NKJV)**. This was not rejection; it was wisdom. He remained present without becoming exposed, open without being unguarded. Discernment allowed Him to steward access without hardening His heart.

Friendly fire is navigated not by emotional withdrawal, but by measured trust. The intercessor learns to remain receptive without becoming vulnerable to unnecessary harm.

Guarding the Heart Without Abandoning Community

Scripture gives clear instruction:
"Keep your heart with all diligence, for out of it spring the issues of life" **(Proverbs 4:23, NKJV).**

Guarding the heart does not mean isolating it. It means stewarding access wisely.

In seasons of prolonged warfare, intercessors may feel compelled to explain themselves, defend their posture, or prove their faithfulness. Yet Scripture does not place the burden of constant explanation on those called to stand. Jesus fulfilled prophecy when He remained silent under accusation:

"He was oppressed and He was afflicted, yet He opened not His mouth" **(Isaiah 53:7, NKJV).**

Not every misunderstanding requires clarification.
Not every offense requires confrontation.

Sometimes restraint is not avoidance, it is obedience.

Community remains essential, but alignment within community matters more than proximity. Scripture records a moment when even apostolic partnership required separation:
"Then the contention became so sharp that they parted from one another" **(Acts 15:39, NKJV).**

Paul and Barnabas did not part as enemies, but as servants stewarding conviction. The Kingdom advanced through both. This reveals a difficult but necessary truth: distance is not always division. At times, it is protection.

How Friendly Fire Develops During Prolonged Warfare

Friendly fire rarely appears at the beginning of warfare.
It develops over time.

Prolonged warfare applies pressure not only to assignments, but to people. When resistance continues without visible resolution, fatigue begins to shape perception. Discernment does not disappear, but it weakens at the edges. Intercessors may still be praying, still standing, still showing up, yet internally, strain begins to accumulate.

In these seasons, unresolved issues surface. Insecurity that was once manageable becomes pronounced. Differences in pace, expression, or calling that were once navigated with grace begin to feel threatening. What is actually the weight of warfare is often misinterpreted as relational offense.

Scripture reflects this pattern. Israel did not murmur at the start of the journey; frustration surfaced when the way became long and familiar (*Numbers 21:4–5*). Prolonged waiting exposed what had not been settled internally. Pressure turned inward before it ever turned outward.

Friendly fire also develops when communication decreases. Fatigue encourages withdrawal, silence, and assumption. Intercessors who once spoke freely begin to guard themselves emotionally. In the absence of clarity, interpretation replaces truth. Misunderstanding hardens into mistrust, not because of malice, but because weariness lowers restraint.

Another factor is unmet expectations. During extended warfare, some expect intensity to produce immediate breakthrough. When results are delayed, disappointment looks for a place to land. If disappointment is not processed before God, it often attaches itself to people. Those who remain standing become targets, not because they are wrong, but because they are present.

Prolonged warfare can also tempt intercessors to police one another's posture. When pressure increases, tolerance decreases. Correction shifts into control. Accountability loses gentleness. What was meant to protect the body begins to wound it.

Perhaps most dangerously, friendly fire develops when spiritual authority is exercised without emotional awareness. Words may be accurate, but timing is ignored. Truth may be correct, but love is absent. Scripture warns that knowledge without love causes damage rather than growth *(1 Corinthians 8:1)*. Accuracy alone does not prevent harm, maturity does.

These patterns do not mean warfare has failed. They mean warfare has lasted long enough to test formation.

Friendly fire is not evidence that the calling is wrong, it is evidence that endurance now requires guarding. If left unrecognized, it quietly accomplishes what external opposition could not. It does not overthrow authority; it isolates it. It does not silence prayer; it fractures the people who carry it.

Understanding how friendly fire develops allows the intercessor to remain sober rather than suspicious, discerning rather than defensive. It invites self-examination before accusation and humility before judgment. Because the goal is not simply to survive warfare, but to remain within it.

Boundaries: Where Responsibility Ends and Trust Begins

Boundaries function quietly, but they preserve strength.

Without boundaries, intercessors absorb what was never assigned to them. They carry emotional weight that belongs to others, assume responsibility God never delegated, and internalize pressure meant to be released in prayer. Over time, this erodes clarity and dulls discernment.

Scripture affirms boundaries through wisdom. *"A prudent man foresees evil and hides himself, but the simple pass on and are punished"* **(Proverbs 22:3, NKJV)**. Boundaries are not fear-based; they are foresight-based. They protect calling without hardening compassion.

Boundaries do not reject people; they define stewardship. They clarify where obedience remains faithful and where overextension becomes harmful. Without them, friendly fire multiplies—not because others intend harm, but because access was never discerned.

Correction Requires Humility and Restraint

Scripture does not dismiss correction, it governs it.

"Brethren, if a man is overtaken in any trespass, you who are spiritual restore such a one in a spirit of gentleness, considering yourself lest you also be tempted" **(Galatians 6:1, NKJV)**.

Correction offered without gentleness becomes control.
Truth delivered without restraint becomes injury.

Friendly fire often occurs not because corrections were wrong, but because posture was misaligned. The goal of correction is restoration, not exposure. When humility is absent, even accurate words wound.

James warns of unrestrained speech:
"If anyone does not stumble in word, he is a perfect man" **(James 3:2, NKJV)**.
Words spoken in warfare carry weight. Without restraint, they fracture trust and weaken unity.

Restraint: The Discipline of Not Engaging Everything

Perhaps the most overlooked safeguard in warfare is restraint.

Scripture reminds us:
"He who has knowledge spares his words" **(Proverbs 17:27, NKJV).**

Not every comment requires response.
Not every tension requires resolution.
Not every wound requires explanation.

Restraint preserves authority. It keeps the intercessor from reacting emotionally and engaging unnecessarily. Jesus often withdrew—not because He lacked power, but because He honored timing and assignment. Silence, in Scripture, is frequently an act of strength.

Friendly fire intensifies when restraint is abandoned—when pressure demands response and emotion dictates engagement. Wisdom teaches the intercessor when to speak, when to stand, and when to remain silent before the Lord.

Leaving Room to Guard the Intercessor

This chapter has not been about assigning blame.
It has been about cultivating maturity.

Friendly fire does not mean warfare has failed. It means warfare has lasted long enough to test formation. Recognizing it allows the intercessor to guard the heart without withdrawing from community, to maintain alignment without hardening, and to remain present without being consumed.

Yet discernment alone is not enough.

If friendly fire is recognized but not guarded against, its effects deepen quietly. This brings us to the next essential work, not confronting others, but guarding oneself.

There are seasons when even those who have carried prayer faithfully for many years, leading, covering, and standing without retreating, discover that endurance requires new wisdom, not because the calling has changed, but because the weight has.

When Friendly Fire Looks Familiar

For many intercessors, these biblical accounts do not feel distant. They feel recognizable.

In modern contexts, friendly fire often surfaces quietly. It may look like a prayer assignment being questioned rather than covered. A discernment being dismissed because it does not align with group expectation. A season of rest interpreted as disengagement. Boundaries mistaken for pride. Silence is labeled as rebellion.

Sometimes it appears in spiritual environments where pressure is high and language is strong. Words spoken "in truth" but without gentleness. Correction offered publicly when privacy was needed. Expectations placed on the intercessor to carry more, pray longer, or endure without acknowledgment of weariness.

In other cases, friendly fire emerges through comparison. One intercessor's expression of prayer becomes the standard by which others are measured. Differences in pace, posture, or assignment are no longer honored but scrutinized. What once felt like unity begins to feel like surveillance.

There are also moments when friendly fire comes through withdrawal rather than words. An intercessor senses distance where connection once existed. Trust feels altered, though no clear offense has been named. The environment becomes unclear, and clarity is replaced with caution.

These experiences are rarely dramatic. They are cumulative.
And because they occur within sacred spaces, they can be deeply disorienting, but do not loose heart intercessor, God is not surprised at the turn of events, He yet remains faithful.

Declaration

- I declare that discernment guards my heart without hardening it.

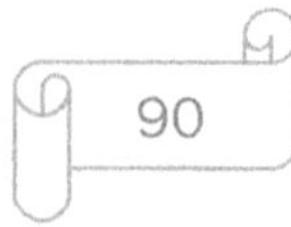

- I declare that internal wounds will not silence my calling or distort my posture.

- I refuse to carry offense that God has not assigned me to bear.

- I choose wisdom over reaction and restraint over retaliation.

- I remain aligned, covered, and clear, even when pressure comes from within.

- I steward my heart, my voice, and my assignment with maturity.

Prayer

Lord, where I have been affected by words, silence, or misunderstanding, heal what has been strained without hardening my heart. Teach me how to remain present, discerning, and aligned.
Guard me from internal erosion and preserve the integrity of my calling. Amen.

Reader Reflection

(Journal or meditate prayerfully)

Take a quiet moment and consider:

- Have I experienced internal strain that I dismissed or minimized?

- Did I respond by withdrawing, overexplaining, or becoming guarded?

- What might wisdom—not emotion—be asking of me in this season?

- How can I remain aligned without absorbing what was never mine to carry?

Let these questions lead you toward clarity, not self-judgment.

Chapter 8: Guarding the Intercessor

Warfare does not end when resistance is confronted. It enters a quieter, more deliberate phase, preservation.

Scripture never portrays preservation as passive. It is intentional, watchful, and wise. Guarding the intercessor is not withdrawal from assignment; it is stewardship of what God has already entrusted. The one who stands in the gap must also be sustained within it.

Many intercessors understand authority but underestimate vulnerability. They know how to engage warfare outwardly yet neglect the quieter work of guarding inwardly. Over time, this imbalance does not remove calling, but it weakens clarity, dulls discernment, and erodes joy. Guarding the intercessor ensures that endurance remains possible without loss.

God's concern is not only that battles are won, but that those who fight them are preserved.

Preservation and Guarding: A Biblical Foundation

In Scripture, preservation speaks to being kept intact over time, not merely protected from destruction, but sustained in strength, clarity, and purpose.

The psalmist declares,
"The Lord shall preserve you from all evil; He shall preserve your soul. The Lord shall preserve your going out and your coming in from this time forth, and even forevermore" **(Psalm 121:7–8, NKJV)**.

Preservation is God's intent, but guarding is the intercessor's responsibility.

To guard in Scripture means to watch over, keep, and tend carefully. It implies awareness and intentionality. Proverbs

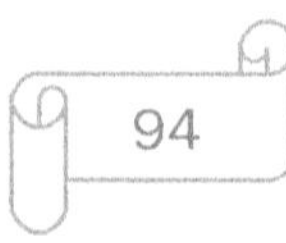

instruct,
"Keep your heart with all diligence, for out of it spring the issues of life" **(Proverbs 4:23, NKJV)**.

Guarding is not fear driven. It is wisdom driven. It acknowledges that what carries authority must also be protected. Scripture never separates calling from care; what God preserves, He also instructs us to guard.

What It Means to Guard (Biblical Language)

When Scripture speaks of guarding, it uses language far richer than simple protection.

In the Old Testament, the primary Hebrew word translated *guard* or *keep* is **shāmar (שָׁמַר)**. This word means *to watch over, to hedge about, to preserve, to attend carefully, and to keep with intention.* It carries the idea of active vigilance, not passive defense. To *shāmar* something is to remain aware, attentive, and responsible for what has been entrusted.

This is the word used in **Proverbs 4:23 (NKJV):**
"Keep (shāmar) your heart with all diligence, for out of it spring the issues of life."

The instruction is not merely to protect the heart from attack, but to **tend it continually**, recognizing its central role in sustaining life, clarity, and calling.

In the New Testament, Scripture often uses the Greek word **phroureō (φρουρέω)**, meaning *to guard by military watch, to garrison, to protect by sentry.* It is a strategic term, one that implies standing watch over something valuable because it is under threat.

Paul uses this word when he writes,
"And the peace of God, which surpasses all understanding, will guard (phroureō) your hearts and minds through Christ Jesus" **(Philippians 4:7, NKJV)**.

This reveals a powerful truth for the intercessor: guarding is not self-effort alone. God's peace itself becomes the sentry. When alignment is maintained, peace stands watch over the inner life, preserving clarity and strength in the midst of warfare.

Together, *shāmar* and *phroureō* form a complete picture. Guarding is both intentional stewardship and divine protection. The intercessor watches carefully, and God stations His peace as defense. Preservation happens where responsibility and grace meet.

To guard, then, is not to withdraw from battle, it is to remain vigilant over what makes endurance possible.

Guarding the Heart

The heart is the center of desire, perception, and response. Scripture consistently emphasizes its importance because what settles in the heart eventually shapes action.

Jesus warned His disciples,
"Take heed to yourselves, lest your hearts be weighed down with carousing, drunkenness, and cares of this life" (Luke 21:34, NKJV).

Cares, not sin, were the threat. Unattended weight dulls sensitivity and clouds discernment. For intercessors, guarding the heart means refusing to allow prolonged warfare, internal erosion, or unmet expectation to take root. It requires regular release of offense, disappointment, and pressure before they harden into posture.

Guarding the Mind

The mind is often the first battleground after prolonged warfare. Scripture instructs believers to tend to think about life intentionally, not passively.

Paul writes,
"Be transformed by the renewing of your mind" **(Romans 12:2,**

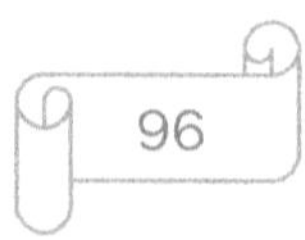

NKJV),
and later adds,
"And the peace of God, which surpasses all understanding, will guard your hearts and minds through Christ Jesus" **(Philippians 4:7, NKJV)**.

Guarding the mind means recognizing when thoughts are being shaped more by pressure than by truth. It requires replacing rumination with renewal and assumption with Scripture. Intercessors who do not guard their thoughts may continue praying accurately while thinking inaccurately, an imbalance that leads to weariness.

Guarding the Spirit

The spirit is the place of communion with God. When the spirit is guarded, sensitivity remains. When it is neglected, prayer becomes mechanical.

Scripture warns,
"He who has no rule over his own spirit is like a city broken down, without walls" **(Proverbs 25:28, NKJV)**.

Guarding the spirit involves honoring boundaries, recognizing limits, and remaining submitted to the Holy Spirit's leading. It means resisting the temptation to override spiritual checks for the sake of urgency or expectation. A guarded spirit remains responsive, not reactive.

Biblical Examples of Guarded Lives

Jesus modeled guarded living without isolation. Though fully available to the Father's will, He did not entrust Himself to everyone:
"Jesus did not commit Himself to them, because He knew all men" **(John 2:24, NKJV)**.
He withdrew when needed, remained silent when appropriate, and spoke only what the Father instructed. His guardedness preserved His clarity and authority.

Paul demonstrates this same wisdom. He openly acknowledged pressure, yet refused to allow it to fracture him internally. He writes,
"We are hard-pressed on every side, yet not crushed... struck down, but not destroyed" **(2 Corinthians 4:8–9, NKJV).**

Paul guarded his inner life through perspective, grace, and alignment with God's strength rather than his own.

Nehemiah offers a powerful picture of guarded leadership in warfare. While rebuilding Jerusalem's walls, he posted watchmen and refused distraction. He responded to opposition with discernment, saying:
"I am doing a great work, so that I cannot come down" **(Nehemiah 6:3, NKJV).**

Nehemiah guarded his focus, his mission, and his spirit—ensuring the work was completed without compromise.

Guarding Through Boundaries

Scripture never equates availability with obedience.
Even Jesus, fully submitted to the Father, did not remain accessible to every demand placed upon Him.

Boundaries are not walls of fear; they are lines of stewardship. They define what the intercessor is assigned to carry and what must be released back to God. Without boundaries, guarding becomes impossible, because exposure remains unchecked.

Nehemiah modeled this clarity when opposition attempted to draw him away from his assignment. His response was firm, not defensive:
"I am doing a great work, so that I cannot come down" **(Nehemiah 6:3, NKJV).**

His refusal was not arrogance, it was alignment. Boundaries preserved the work and the worker.

For the intercessor, boundaries may include:

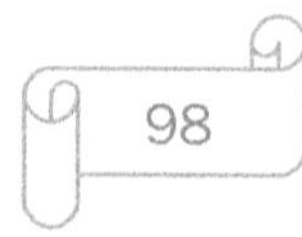

- Saying no to unassigned burdens

- Limiting access during seasons of warfare

- Releasing responsibility for outcomes God has not entrusted

These are not acts of disengagement. They are acts of obedience.

Guarding Through Rest

Rest is not the opposite of warfare; it is part of its design.

God Himself established rest as holy rhythm, not reward. Scripture instructs:
"In returning and rest you shall be saved; in quietness and confidence shall be your strength" **(Isaiah 30:15, NKJV).**

For the intercessor, rest is not inactivity, it is recalibration. It restores discernment, renews strength, and protects the spirit from becoming driven rather than led.

Even Jesus withdrew repeatedly, not because He lacked power, but because He honored the Father's rhythm. *"So He Himself often withdrew into the wilderness and prayed"* **(Luke 5:16, NKJV).**

Rest guards the intercessor from mistaking endurance for faithfulness and exhaustion for obedience.

Guarding Through Submission to God's Covering

The deepest form of guarding is submission, not to pressure, expectation, or urgency, but to God's covering.

Submission acknowledges that authority flows downward, not upward. When the intercessor operates outside of God's covering, whether through independence, overextension, or self-imposed burden, guarding collapses.

Scripture promises protection within divine alignment:
"He who dwells in the secret place of the Most High shall abide under the shadow of the Almighty" **(Psalm 91:1, NKJV).**

Covering is not created through effort. It is entered through surrender.

Submission keeps the intercessor positioned, under God's voice, under His timing, and under His restraint. It allows warfare to be sustained without consuming the one who carries it.

Why This Matters

Boundaries guard capacity.
Rest guards clarity.
Submission guards authority.

Without these, even disciplined intercessors may continue praying while quietly losing peace, joy, and discernment. God's design has never been that the intercessor be depleted in order to be effective.

He guards what He calls, when it is submitted to Him.

The Work of Guarding

Guarding the intercessor is not about becoming closed in and isolated, it is about becoming clear. It allows the heart to remain soft, the mind to remain sound, and the spirit to remain responsive.

This chapter does not call the intercessor to disengage from warfare.
It calls them to remain whole within it. Guarding the intercessor is not an end in itself. It ensures that what God establishes through prayer can be maintained without collapse.

Only a guarded intercessor can steward territory without losing alignment. Guarding the intercessor is not the final aim.
It ensures that what has been preserved can now be entrusted with greater responsibility.

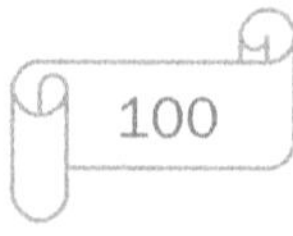

With heart, mind, and spirit aligned, the work shifts from protection to expansion. We now turn to the work of establishing territory, without losing what God has preserved.

Prayer

Father,
I place my calling under Your covering.
Teach me to guard what You have entrusted without fear or striving.
Show me where to set boundaries, when to rest, and how to remain submitted to Your timing.
Preserve my heart, renew my mind, and steady my spirit.
Let my strength be sustained by alignment, not effort.
In Jesus' Name, Amen.

Declaration

- I declare that my calling is preserved by God and stewarded with wisdom.

- I set boundaries according to assignment, not pressure.

- I receive rest as a holy rhythm, not a reward for exhaustion.

- I remain submitted to God's covering and timing.

- I guard my heart, mind, and spirit with discernment and peace.

- I endure in warfare without losing clarity, joy, or alignment.

Reader Reflection

(Journal or meditate prayerfully)

- Where might I be overextended beyond my assignment?

- Have I made a mistake for constant availability for obedience?

- What boundaries might God be inviting me to establish in this season?

- Do I allow myself to rest without guilt, trusting God's covering?

- What would guarding my inner life look like practically right now?

Let these questions draw you toward alignment, not self-correction.

A Prophetic Word to God's Intercessors

As you delve into these pages, I sense the Lord is doing something new within you. He is anchoring you deeply and deliberately, so that you do not drift backward or lose ground. Where instability once threatened progress, God is now establishing firmness. This is not a season of retreat; it is a season of acceleration.

I hear the Spirit say that He is filling you anew with hope, peace, and joy, beyond what you have known before. There is a strengthening taking place, an inner restoration where weariness once lingered. The Lord is healing places shaped by past trauma, disappointment, and prolonged warfare. I see Him removing old smoke screens and residual haze from former seasons, clarifying vision, lifting heaviness, and restoring clarity of mind and heart.

The call is clear: arise and move in the governance God has placed upon you. What once felt restrained is now being released. I see a renewed outlook, on life, on yourself, and even in how you perceive God. Perspective is being healed. Capacity is being enlarged.

The Lord says there is still much for you to accomplish in the earth. You are not nearing the end, you are stepping into deeper purpose. With long life, He will satisfy you and show you, His salvation. What felt delayed has not been denied; it has been preserved.

And hear this clearly: when you open your mouth in alignment with His will, God is ready to move on your words. Your prayers are not falling to the ground. They are being received, weighed, and released in their appointed time.

All things are becoming new.

Stand steady. Remain anchored.
And govern from the place God has prepared for you.

Says, the Spirit of Lord!

Chapter 9: Establishing Territory

Preservation prepares the intercessor for expansion.

Once the heart is guarded, the mind renewed, and the spirit aligned, prayer moves beyond defense. The work of the intercessor does not end with surviving warfare; it advances toward establishing what God has already declared. Scripture names this progression clearly. It speaks of possession, inheritance, and dominion, distinct yet connected realities that describe how God's purposes move from promise into permanence.

Possession in Scripture refers to taking hold of what has already been given by divine decree. God repeatedly told Israel that the land was theirs before they ever set foot in it. Possession required obedience, movement, and endurance, not permission. It was not earned through effort but activated through faith. For the intercessor, possession means moving beyond acknowledgment of promise into consistent engagement with what God has authorized. Prayer no longer asks *if* God will move; it aligns with *where* He has already granted access.

Joshua 1:3 (NKJV)
"Every place that the sole of your foot will tread upon I have given you."

Deuteronomy 11:24 (NKJV)
"Every place on which the sole of your foot treads shall be yours."

Hebrews 11:8 (NKJV)
"By faith Abraham obeyed when he was called to go out... not knowing where he was going."

Inheritance speaks to continuity. It is not merely about receiving something, but about stewarding it across time. Inheritance in Scripture is tied to lineage, responsibility, and preservation. What

is inherited must be guarded, cultivated, and passed forward. For the intercessor, inheritance includes spiritual authority, generational breakthrough, and covenant promises that outlive personal experience. Establishing territory means praying not only for present manifestation, but for sustained order that remains beyond one season or one life.

Genesis 17:7–8 (NKJV)

"I will establish My covenant... for an everlasting covenant... and I will give to you and your descendants... the land."

Hebrews 6:12 (NKJV)

"Those who through faith and patience inherit the promises."

Dominion describes governance. It is the ability to rule, maintain order, and exercise authority under God's direction. Dominion is never independent power; it is delegated authority expressed through alignment. Scripture presents dominion as stewardship rather than control. For the intercessor, dominion emerges when prayer shifts from confrontation to governance—when the focus becomes maintaining truth, reinforcing alignment, and ensuring that what God has established remains ordered and undisturbed.

Genesis 1:26 (NKJV)

"Let them have dominion... over all the earth."

Luke 19:17 (NKJV)

"Because you were faithful in a very little, have authority over ten cities."

Revelation 5:10 (NKJV)

"And have made us kings and priests... and we shall reign on the earth."

Together, possession, inheritance, and dominion describe the full scope of territorial prayer. Possession takes hold. Inheritance sustains. Dominion governs. Establishing territory requires all three. Without possession, promise remains theoretical. Without

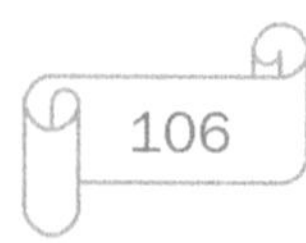

inheritance, breakthrough becomes temporary. Without dominion, territory remains vulnerable to reoccupation

To establish territory is not to claim something new, but to occupy what God has already given authority to steward. It is the difference between breakthrough and maintenance. Breakthrough opens the door; territory keeps it open. Prayer shifts from confronting resistance to sustaining order.

For the intercessor, establishing territory means praying in a way that maintains spiritual ground—ensuring that what God has released is not reclaimed by the enemy through neglect, compromise, or misalignment.

What It Means to Establish Territory (Biblical Understanding)

In Scripture, territory is not merely geographic; it is spiritual authority expressed in lived reality. God repeatedly promised land, influence, and inheritance, but possession required obedience, endurance, and continued alignment.

The Lord told Joshua:
"Every place that the sole of your foot will tread upon I have given you" **(Joshua 1:3, NKJV).**

The land was already given, yet it had to be walked. Authority had been granted, but it had to be exercised. Territory was established not through awareness of promise alone, but through faithful occupation.

For the intercessor, this reveals a critical truth:
what God promises must be stewarded after warfare ends.

God may have spoken a promise over your life, through Scripture, prophetic confirmation, or a quiet conviction planted in your spirit. You may have received a word concerning your family line, your calling, or your future assignment. For some, that word involved provision and increase, an instruction to steward wealth with wisdom, to build a business, or to establish something that would extend beyond personal gain. For others, it was a generational declaration: that cycles of poverty, limitation, or instability would end with them.

Whatever God has spoken, that declaration represents territory already granted. Heaven has issued the authorization. Yet many intercessors discover that receiving the word is only the beginning. Opposition often follows promise. Resistance arises not because the word was unclear, but because possession must be established.

Scripture makes this pattern plain:
"Every place that the sole of your foot will tread upon I have given you" **(Joshua 1:3, NKJV).**

The land was given before it was occupied. Authority was granted before it was exercised. Establishing territory, then, is the work of moving from promise into possession.

In matters of wealth and provision, Scripture adds important clarity. God declares,
"And you shall remember the Lord your God, for it is He who gives you power to get wealth, that He may establish His covenant" **(Deuteronomy 8:18, NKJV).**

Scripture deepens this understanding when it speaks of wealth and power in covenant terms. In Deuteronomy 8:18, the word translated *power* is the Hebrew **kōaḥ**, meaning strength, capacity, and sustained ability. It refers not merely to physical strength, but to God-given endurance, the internal capacity to produce, manage, and steward increase without collapse. The word translated *wealth* is **ḥayil**, a term that encompasses far more than money. It speaks of resources, strength, efficiency, and even valor. It is the same word used to describe mighty warriors and capable leaders.

Together, these words reveal that God does not simply bestow wealth; He entrusts capacity. He gives the ability (*kōaḥ*) to generate and steward resources (*ḥayil*) so that His covenant may

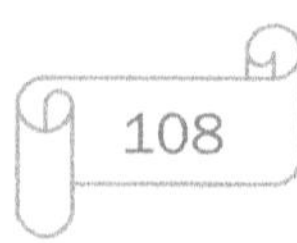

be established. Wealth, then, is not an end in itself, but a means of governance. It is territory granted for purpose, not accumulation.

For the intercessor, this reframes financial and marketplace resistance. Opposition in these areas is rarely about money alone; it is about covenant stewardship. When God assigns territory connected to provision, influence, or generational shift, resistance often rises to contest the capacity required to carry it. Establishing territory in this context means remaining aligned long enough for capacity to mature, so that increase does not outpace character, and expansion does not exceed submission.

This is why Scripture warns the people to *remember the Lord*. Forgetfulness leads to misattributing capacity to self and resources to entitlement. Remembrance keeps territory governed. When the intercessor remains submitted, *kōaḥ* is sustained and *ḥayil* is directed, allowing covenant purpose, not self-effort, to define the outcome.

Establishing territory, then, is not merely taking ground. It is stewarding capacity under God's authority so that what is built endures.

Again, this reveals that financial territory is never granted merely for personal advancement. Wealth, influence, and resource are entrusted so that God's covenant may be established and sustained. When resistance arises in the marketplace or in provision, it is often because territory tied to covenant purpose is being contested.

In generational matters, establishing territory means standing firm until old patterns lose their authority. In marketplace assignments, it means continuing to build even when progress is slow or opposed. In both cases, stagnation does not indicate failure; it reveals contested ground.

Establishing territory requires governed persistence. It is refusing to live indefinitely at the edge of fulfillment, aware of the promise, yet hesitant to occupy it. God provides what is needed at the moment of promise, but the intercessor must remain aligned long enough for that provision to take root, mature, and endure.

This is not passive waiting.
It is faithful stewardship.

Biblical Examples:

David Establishing the Kingdom

David was anointed king long before he ruled in peace. Once established in Jerusalem, Scripture records that
"David went on and became great, and the Lord God of hosts was with him" **(2 Samuel 5:10, NKJV).**

David secured Jerusalem, defeated remaining resistance, and brought the ark of the covenant into the center of governance. Spiritual order and leadership alignment followed military victory.

For the intercessor, this shows that territory is established when God's presence is enthroned, not merely acknowledged.

Nehemiah Rebuilding and Guarding

Nehemiah's work did not end with rebuilding walls. Guards were posted. Watches were established. People were positioned by families and sections.

Scripture says,
"Those who built on the wall... held a weapon in one hand and worked with the other" **(Nehemiah 4:17, NKJV).**

This is territory language. The work was protected while it was being completed. Establishing territory requires vigilance after progress.

Paul Establishing Spiritual Territory

In Ephesus, Paul remained for two years, teaching daily, confronting false authority, and strengthening believers. Scripture records:
"So the word of the Lord grew mightily and prevailed" **(Acts 19:20, NKJV).**

Paul did not merely cast out resistance; he remained long enough for truth to take root. Territory was established through sustained teaching, alignment, and order.

For the intercessor, this reveals that territory is secured when truth governs the atmosphere.

What Establishing Territory Looks Like for the Intercessor

For the intercessor, establishing territory includes:

- Praying for maintenance (the ability to maintain), not just breakthrough

- Interceding for order, structure, and alignment after deliverance

- Standing watch so spiritual ground is not reclaimed

- Sustaining prayer that reinforces truth where resistance once stood

Territory is established when prayer shifts from confrontation to stewardship.

This phase of warfare requires maturity. There is less intensity, but greater responsibility. Less spectacle, but more endurance. The intercessor learns that not all victories are loud, and not all warfare is urgent.

A Sobering Reality

Scripture shows that unguarded territory is vulnerable territory. Israel lost ground when obedience faded. Churches struggled when doctrine weakened. Leaders fell when vigilance lapsed.

Establishing territory requires the same discernment that won the battle, and often more restraint.

This is why guarding the intercessor mattered. Only a preserved intercessor can maintain what God has established without losing alignment.

Breaking Systems to Secure Possession

Below are the primary systems Scripture reveals that intercessors are often assigned to confront when territory is being established, especially in generational, financial, and marketplace contexts.

1. Systems of Poverty and Lack

These are not simply financial shortages but mindsets and structures that normalize insufficiency, dependence, and limitation.

Scripture warns Israel that poverty can become systemic when God's covenant provision is forgotten:

"Beware lest you forget the Lord your God... and say in your heart, 'My power and the might of my hand have gained me this wealth.'" **(Deuteronomy 8:11–18, NKJV)**

Intercessors often confront:

- Cycles of debt and financial instability passed through generations

- Fear-based decision-making that resists growth

- A theology that equates humility with lack

Establishing territory here means dismantling the belief systems and agreements that oppose God's provision and replacing them with covenant truth.

2. Systems of Fear and Control

Fear is one of the most entrenched governing systems in Scripture. It resists movement, obedience, and expansion.

God told Joshua repeatedly,

"Be strong and of good courage... do not be afraid, nor be dismayed" **(Joshua 1:9, NKJV).**

Fear-based systems appear as:

- Control masquerading as wisdom

- Delay justified as caution

- Obedience postponed until conditions feel safe

Intercessors must confront fear not emotionally but authoritatively refusing to allow it to dictate timing or obedience.

3. Systems of Identity Distortion

Strongholds often remain because identity has been shaped more by history than by truth.

Paul writes,

"Do not be conformed to this world, but be transformed by the renewing of your mind" **(Romans 12:2, NKJV).**

These systems manifest as:

- Generational labels ("this is just how our family is")

- Internalized failure or inferiority

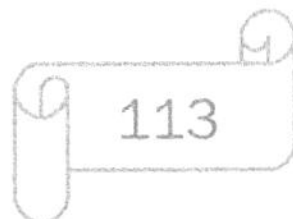

- Calling diminished by past trauma

Establishing territory here requires sustained truth-based intercession until identity aligns with heaven's declaration.

4. Systems of Religious Formalism

Not all resistance is overtly sinful. Some are preserved through structure without Spirit.

Jesus confronted this system repeatedly, saying,

"These people draw near to Me with their mouth... but their heart is far from Me" **(Matthew 15:8, NKJV).**

Religious systems resist territory by:

- Valuing routine over obedience

- Replacing discernment with tradition

- Policing form while neglecting fruit

Intercessors must dismantle false order that resist transformation while appearing holy.

5. Systems of Delay and Stagnation

Some systems are built entirely around postponement, the promise acknowledged but never possessed.

The writer of Hebrews warns against this posture:

"That you do not become sluggish, but imitate those who through faith and patience inherit the promises" **(Hebrews 6:12, NKJV).**

These systems manifest as:

- Endless preparation without execution

- Waiting for confirmation after obedience is already clear

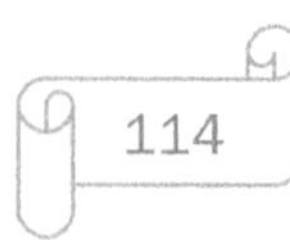

- Movement replaced by discussion

Establishing territory requires recognizing when patience has shifted into paralysis.

6. Systems of Silence and Passivity

Silence can be strategic, but prolonged silence in the face of assignment becomes resistance.

God rebuked Israel through the prophets for failing to speak when justice was required:

"Cry aloud, spare not; lift up your voice like a trumpet" **(Isaiah 58:1, NKJV).**

Intercessors often must confront:

- Fear of visibility

- Spiritual intimidation

- Internal agreements to stay hidden

Territory is never established through silence alone.

A Necessary Clarification

Intercessors are not assigned to dismantle every system they discern.

Scripture is clear:

"The weapons of our warfare are not carnal but mighty in God for pulling down strongholds" **(2 Corinthians 10:4, NKJV).**

Only assigned systems are meant to be confronted. Discernment reveals many things; authority engages only what God authorizes. When intercessors attempt to dismantle unassigned systems, fatigue increases and impact diminishes.

The Purpose of Confrontation

Systems are not destroyed for the sake of conflict.
They are dismantled so territory can be governed by truth.

Establishing territory means replacing resistance with order, confusion with clarity, and opposition with stewardship.

This is why guarding the intercessor mattered.
And this is why precision preceded engagement.

Because territory is not taken through force,
but through alignment that outlasts resistance.

Prayer

Father,
I thank You for the territory You have entrusted to me—
what has been promised, what has been fought for, and what must now be stewarded. Teach me to govern with humility and vigilance. Help me to possess what You have given, preserve what You have established, and exercise dominion without pride or neglect.
Keep my heart aligned, my discernment sharp, and my obedience steady. Let what You establish through my prayers endure beyond this season. Amen.

Declaration

- I declare that I possess what God has already authorized.

- I steward my inheritance with faith, patience, and obedience.

- I govern territory through alignment, not force.

- I refuse drift, complacency, and compromise.

- I maintain what God has established with vigilance and humility.

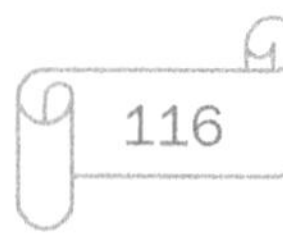

- I exercise dominion as a faithful steward under God's authority.

Reader Reflection

(Journal or meditate prayerfully)

- What territory has God already entrusted to me—spiritually, generationally, or in the marketplace?

- Am I stewarding this territory with vigilance, or have I grown familiar with it?

- Where might God be calling me to move from breakthrough into governance?

- What practices help me maintain alignment after victory?

- How can I ensure that what God establishes through me will endure?

Let this reflection lead you toward stewardship, not pressure, clarity, not striving.

Quiet Transition Forward

Territory reveals readiness,
but commissioning requires trust.

The intercessor who can steward authority without drifting
is prepared to carry it beyond themselves.

We now turn to the final shaping:
the intercessor who is commissioned, not merely to contend,
but to govern faithfully what God has established.

Chapter 10: The Commissioned Intercessor

What It Means to Be Commissioned

To be commissioned is to be sent with authority and responsibility. In Scripture, commissioning is never merely an assignment; it is an entrustment. God does not commission people to explore possibilities, He commissions them to carry weight. Commissioning signifies that Heaven has determined the vessel can be trusted to steward influence without losing alignment.

Biblically, commissioning always follows preparation. The Scriptures consistently reveals that commissioning is not granted at the moment of calling, but at the point of readiness. Calling identifies purpose; commissioning entrusts responsibility. God often reveals intention long before He releases authority, not to delay fulfillment, but to protect both the work and the worker.

Throughout Scripture, calling is frequently disclosed early, while commissioning follows seasons of formation. Joseph received dreams as a youth, but authority came after years of refinement, testing, and endurance. David was anointed king in obscurity, yet commissioned to rule only after faithfulness was proven through hidden battles and restraint under pressure. Even Jesus, fully aware of His identity, did not begin public ministry until the Father affirmed Him at baptism and the Spirit led Him through testing in the wilderness.

These patterns reveal a consistent principle: readiness is not measured by awareness, gifting, or desire, but by alignment, obedience, and endurance. Commissioning requires the ability to carry authority without misusing it, to endure opposition without losing posture, and to steward influence without becoming independent. What is revealed in calling must be stabilized through formation before it can be released through commissioning.

God withholds commissioning not because He withholds trust, but because He values preservation. Authority released prematurely often fractures the vessel meant to carry it. Scripture demonstrates that weight precedes responsibility, and responsibility demands maturity. Commissioning waits until the intercessor can govern what God gives without being governed by it.

This distinction guards the intercessor from confusion. Delay is not denial. Waiting is not failure. The space between calling and commissioning is where obedience is refined, discernment is sharpened, and character is anchored. It is here that the intercessor learns how to stand without being seen, remain faithful without affirmation, and submit without certainty.

When readiness is complete, commissioning does not require striving or announcement. It arrives with clarity, authority, and peace. Heaven sends when the vessel is prepared to carry what has been promised, not only to receive it, but to sustain it.

To be commissioned is to move from *potential* into *responsibility*. The intercessor is no longer simply responding to burden; they are carrying authority. Prayer becomes less about discovery and more about enforcement. The commissioned intercessor understands that authority is not proven by volume or intensity, but by obedience, restraint, and endurance.

Commissioning does not elevate position, it deepens accountability.

The Marks of a Commissioned Intercessor

A commissioned intercessor carries distinct characteristics shaped by formation rather than ambition.

First, they operate from clarity rather than urgency. Their prayers are measured, not reactive. They do not engage in every issue they discern, because commissioning teaches discernment of assignment. They understand that authority is effective only within God's authorization.

Second, they carry weight without striving. There is steadiness in their posture. They have learned how to endure without burning out and how to govern without control. Their confidence rests in alignment, not outcome.

Third, a commissioned intercessor demonstrates obedient restraint. They know when to speak and when to remain silent, when to confront and when to wait. They do not feel compelled to prove authority; authority speaks through consistency.

Fourth, they remain submitted to God's covering and the ministry God plants them in. Commissioning does not remove dependence, it deepens it. The commissioned intercessor stays yielded to God's timing, voice, and correction. They recognize that independence erodes authority, while submission sustains it.

Finally, they understand that commissioning is not about visibility, but stewardship. They are trusted with atmosphere, alignment, and territory, not for personal distinction, but for covenant purposes.

Biblical Models of Commissioning:

Jeremiah: Commissioned Through Formation, Not Confidence

Jeremiah's calling was declared early, even before birth. God spoke with unmistakable clarity:
"Before I formed you in the womb I knew you; before you were born, I sanctified you; I ordained you a prophet to the nations" **(Jeremiah 1:5, NKJV).**

Yet calling did not equal readiness. Jeremiah immediately responded with hesitation, aware of his youth and inadequacy. His reaction reveals an important truth: awareness of calling does not automatically confer capacity to carry it. God did not withdraw the calling, nor did He rush Jeremiah into full authority. Instead, He established the terms of commissioning.

"Do not say, 'I am a youth,' for you shall go to all to whom I send you, and whatever I command you, you shall speak" **(Jeremiah 1:7, NKJV).**

Commissioning followed clarity of submission. God defined Jeremiah's assignment and then touched his mouth, symbolically transferring authority that Jeremiah could not generate on his own. Only then did God articulate the scope of his commission:
"See, I have this day set you over the nations and over the kingdoms, to root out and to pull down, to destroy and to throw down, to build and to plant" **(Jeremiah 1:10, NKJV).**

Jeremiah's life demonstrates that commissioning requires more than calling, it requires readiness to speak what God commands, remain faithful when resisted, and endure without losing posture. His authority was released not because he felt ready, but because God knew he would remain aligned under pressure.

Isaiah: Commissioned After Purification and Surrender

Isaiah's commissioning reveals the same principle through a different path. His call unfolded not through prophetic declaration first, but through encounter. In the presence of God's holiness, Isaiah became acutely aware of his own insufficiency:
"Woe is me, for I am undone" **(Isaiah 6:5, NKJV).**

Before Isaiah was sent, he was cleansed. A coal from the altar touched his lips, symbolizing purification, alignment, and readiness. Only after this moment did the question of commissioning arise:
"Whom shall I send, and who will go for Us?" **(Isaiah 6:8, NKJV).**

Isaiah's response, *"Here am I! Send me"* did not emerge from ambition, but from surrender. He was not commissioned because

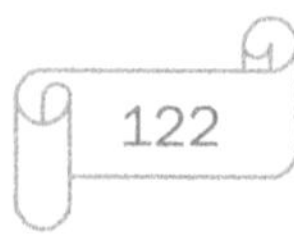

he desired the role, but because he was willing to carry it without condition. God entrusted him with a message that would be difficult to receive and slow to bear fruit. Commissioning came not with assurance of success, but with expectation of faithfulness.

Isaiah's experience reveals that readiness involves purification and consent. Authority is released only after the heart has been aligned to speak what God says, regardless of outcome.

The Pattern Revealed

Both Jeremiah and Isaiah confirm the same truth: commissioning follows readiness, not revelation. Calling may be disclosed early, but authority is released only when the vessel can endure the weight attached to it. God does not commission prematurely because He values preservation over speed. Authority given before formation fractures the carrier; responsibility released before maturity compromises the assignment.

This is why Scripture presents delay not as denial, but as preparation. The space between calling and commissioning is where obedience is refined, discernment is sharpened, and character is anchored. It is where the intercessor learns how to remain faithful without affirmation and aligned without certainty.

When commissioning comes, it does not require striving or announcement. It arrives with clarity, authority, and peace, because readiness has already been established.

How Commissioning Reshapes Prayer Posture and Responsibility

Commissioning does not make prayer more intense; it makes it more consequential. Intensity expends energy in the moment, but consequences carry weight over time. Before commissioning, prayer often rises in response to pressure, urgent, fervent, and necessary for formation. After commissioning, prayer is no longer driven by immediacy; it is governed by responsibility.

When an intercessor is commissioned, their prayers do not simply address circumstances, they shape outcomes. Words spoken in prayer begin to establish patterns that others will live within. Decisions made in prayer affect environments, seasons, and trajectories. The intercessor becomes aware that prayer is no longer only a means of engagement, but an instrument of governance.

This is why commissioned prayer requires restraint as much as boldness. The intercessor understands that speaking carries consequences, and silence carries consequences as well. Prayer is weighed before it is released. It is no longer fueled by urgency alone, but by discernment and submission. What is prayed must be sustainable, not merely effective.

Commissioned prayer also carries responsibility for aftermath. The intercessor becomes accountable not just for what shifts, but for what remains aligned after the shift. Intense prayer can move something quickly; consequential prayer ensures that what moves does not collapse or drift once the moment passes.

A clear biblical example of responsibility for what remains after prayer is answered and accountability for maintenance, not just movement, is found in Nehemiah after the walls of Jerusalem were rebuilt.

Nehemiah's story is often celebrated for breakthrough, but Scripture is just as intentional about what happened *after* the breakthrough.

After intense prayer, fasting, confrontation, and endurance, the wall was completed in record time. Scripture records the moment of victory plainly:

"So the wall was finished... in fifty-two days."
(Nehemiah 6:15, NKJV)

The movement was undeniable. Resistance was overcome. The work was done.
But Nehemiah did not treat completion as conclusion.

Immediately after the prayer was answered and the wall stood, Nehemiah shifted from builder to governor. Scripture says:

"Then it was, when the wall was built... that I gave the charge of Jerusalem to my brother Hanani... for he was a faithful man and feared God more than many."
(Nehemiah 7:1–2, NKJV)

This is the moment of accountability.

Nehemiah understood that answered prayer created responsibility, not just relief. The wall did not secure the city on its own. Gates had to be watched. Leadership had to be appointed. Systems had to be established. Scripture notes that the gates were not to be opened until the sun was high, and guards were assigned by families and locations (Nehemiah 7:3). Prayer had produced movement, but maintenance required governance.

This reveals a vital truth for the intercessor:
what prayer establishes must be protected by order.

Nehemiah did not continue confronting enemies at the same intensity. Instead, he instituted structure. He understood that spiritual breakthroughs without sustained vigilance invite re-entry. The responsibility of leadership did not end when prayer succeeded; it increased.

Another layer of accountability appears later when Nehemiah returned and discovered compromise had crept back into the city, alliances reformed, boundaries loosened, worship neglected (Nehemiah 13). The wall still stood, but alignment had drifted. Nehemiah's response shows that maintenance is ongoing, not automatic.

This example captures the essence of commissioned responsibility:

- Prayer moved the work forward.

- Authority maintained the outcome.

- Accountability remained even after success.

Nehemiah teaches that commissioning is not proven by how powerfully one prays in crisis, but by how faithfully one governs after God answers.

For the intercessor, this means answered prayer is not an ending, it is an entrustment. Movement requires faith. Maintenance requires maturity. And Heaven holds the commissioned intercessor accountable not only for breakthrough, but for what is allowed to stand afterward.

This is the weight of commissioning:
to pray until God moves and then to steward what remains.

This weight does not elevate the intercessor, it humbles them. Consequential prayer demands maturity, patience, and continued dependence on God. Authority is no longer proven by volume or duration, but by faithfulness and alignment. The intercessor learns that not every burden must be carried vocally, and not every moment requires declaration.

In this way, commissioning refines prayer. It moves it from expression to stewardship, from reaction to responsibility. Prayer becomes less about how forcefully one engages and more about how faithfully one governs what God has entrusted.

This is the quiet gravity of commissioning: prayer that does not merely contend, but shapes what endures.

Nehemiah shows us responsibility after breakthrough at the level of governance and structure. But commissioning also reshapes how prayer functions at the level of covenant and intercession itself.

Another clear biblical picture of this truth can be seen in Moses' prayer life before and after commissioning.

Before Moses was commissioned, his prayers were often urgent and reactive, shaped by pressure and immediate threat. At the Red Sea, Moses cried out to God as fear and crisis closed in. The people were panicking, Pharaoh was advancing, and death seemed imminent. His prayer rose from necessity and desperation. Yet God's response revealed that Moses was standing at the threshold of a shift:

"Why do you cry to Me? Tell the children of Israel to go forward."
(Exodus 14:15, NKJV)

At this moment, Moses was still learning authority. Prayer was intense, necessary, and formative, but it had not yet become fully consequential. God was teaching Moses that crying out was no longer enough; responsibility now required action aligned with authority.

After commissioning, Moses' prayer posture changed.

Once Moses had been established as leader, mediator, and covenant steward, his prayers were no longer primarily reactive. They became governing prayers, shaping outcomes for generations. When Israel sinned with the golden calf, Moses did not panic or plead in fear. He stood before God with covenant awareness and interceded with weight:

"Yet now, if You will forgive their sin, but if not, I pray, blot me out of Your book which You have written."
(Exodus 32:32, NKJV)

This prayer was not intense, it was consequential. Moses understood that his intercession would determine the nation's future. His prayer carried generational impact, not momentary

relief. God relented, not because of emotional fervor, but because Moses was praying from covenant responsibility.

This progression from urgency to authority is not limited to leadership figures alone. It is the pattern Scripture presents even in the life of Christ Himself.

Before public commissioning, Jesus spent nights in prayer, fasting, and seeking the Father's will (Luke 6:12). These prayers were formative, shaping obedience, submission, and alignment. After commissioning, His prayers became measured, purposeful, and weight-bearing. In John 17, Jesus did not pray urgently or emotionally. He prayed deliberately, addressing future generations, spiritual authority, unity, and preservation:

"I do not pray for these alone, but also for those who will believe in Me through their word."
(John 17:20, NKJV)

This prayer did not move crowds in the moment, but it has governed the Church for centuries. It is one of the most consequential prayers ever spoken.

These examples reveal the pattern Scripture consistently presents,
before commissioning, prayer is shaped by pressure and formation; after commissioning, prayer is shaped by responsibility and stewardship. Intensity gives way to authority. Urgency gives way to governance. The intercessor is no longer learning how to pray, they are carrying the weight of what prayer establishes.

This is why commissioning does not make prayer louder or longer. It makes it matter longer.

Prayer

Father,
I acknowledge that calling is Your gift, but commissioning is Your

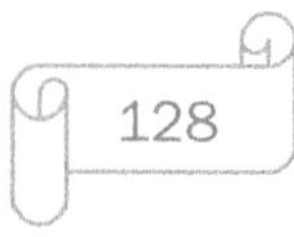

trust. I yield myself not only to what You have revealed, but to what You are entrusting. Teach me to carry authority without striving and responsibility without fear.

Guard my alignment as You increase my influence. Train my spirit to steward what You establish through prayer, and to remain faithful after the breakthrough comes.

I receive the weight of commissioning with humility, knowing that You send only what You have prepared. Let my prayers shape what endures, and let my obedience sustain what You move. Amen.

Declaration

I declare that I am not only called—I am being prepared.

- I receive commissioning as responsibility, not elevation.

- I steward authority with obedience and restraint.

- I pray with awareness of consequence, not urgency alone.

- I remain aligned after breakthrough, not just during warfare.

- I govern what God establishes without striving to control it.

- I remain submitted so that my authority remains intact.

What God entrusts, I will steward.
What prayer establishes, I will maintain.
I am commissioned for faithfulness, not visibility.

Reader Reflection

(Journal or meditate prayerfully)

Take a moment to consider these questions quietly before the Lord:

- Am I more focused on breakthrough, or on stewardship after breakthrough?

- Have I equated calling with readiness, or allowed God to form me fully?

- How has my prayer life shifted as responsibility has increased?

- Am I prepared to maintain what God establishes through my intercession?

Commissioning is not proven by how powerfully one prays in crisis, but by how faithfully one governs after God answers.

Sit with this truth.
Let it settle.
Let it shape your posture moving forward.

Chapter 11: Warfare Wisdom

Warfare does not end for the intercessor; it matures. In Scripture, warfare is not a temporary assignment but an apostolic reality, a lifelong engagement that shapes calling, authority, and responsibility. The intercessor does not graduate out of warfare, but they do grow into wisdom concerning it. What changes is not the presence of conflict, but the posture from which it is engaged.

Wisdom in warfare is not gained through avoidance, but through endurance. It is formed by what has been confronted, survived, and stewarded over time. Scripture does not glorify endless battle; it honors those who learn how to discern its seasons, boundaries, and purposes. The intercessor who has walked through prolonged resistance begins to recognize that not all warfare is meant to be fought with the same intensity, nor engaged in the same way.

This is why Scripture can declare, *"Speak comfort to Jerusalem, and cry out to her, that her warfare is accomplished"* (Isaiah 40:2). This statement does not suggest that opposition has ceased forever. Rather, it announces that a specific season of contention has fulfilled its purpose. Judgment has run its course. Correction has achieved its aim. What needed to be confronted has been confronted, and wisdom now governs what comes next.

Isaiah's prophecy reveals a crucial truth: some warfare is instructional, not perpetual. God allows seasons of battle to refine alignment, restore order, and prepare His people for a different posture, one no longer driven by correction, but by restoration. Warfare being "accomplished" signals a transition from contending to rebuilding, from resisting to establishing.

This pattern appears throughout Scripture. David spent years engaged in relentless warfare, both external and internal. Yet later, he acknowledged that God had given him wisdom through those battles. When Solomon ascended the throne, Scripture notes that *"the Lord gave Solomon wisdom and exceedingly great understanding"* **(1 Kings 4:29, NKJV)**. Solomon did not inherit a kingdom in chaos, but one stabilized by David's warfare and governed by wisdom. The sword prepared the ground; wisdom maintained it.

Paul's apostolic life reflects this same reality. He described his ministry as warfare *"I fight, not as one who beats the air"* **(1 Corinthians 9:26, NKJV)**, yet his letters reveal a man who had learned discernment, restraint, and timing. Paul did not engage in every conflict directly. At times he confronted; at times he endured; at times he withdrew. His wisdom was not the absence of battle, but the fruit of having walked through it faithfully.

Even Jesus demonstrated warfare wisdom. He confronted demonic resistance openly, yet He also withdrew from crowds, refused premature engagement, and declined to respond to every provocation. His authority was unquestioned, but His restraint was deliberate. He understood that wisdom is not passive, it is discerning participation in the Father's will.

Warfare wisdom, then, is not disengagement. It is informed engagement. It recognizes that warfare is an apostolic career, woven into the life of the intercessor, but also acknowledges that God does not intend His people to remain locked in the same battles forever. Some wars teach obedience. Others establish authority. Still others prepare the ground for dominion.

This chapter is written for the intercessor who has learned through experience that constant warfare without wisdom can erode what prayer has already established. Wisdom does not remove vigilance; it refines it. It teaches when to contend, when to stand, and when to allow God's completed work to speak for itself.

Warfare continues.
But it is now governed by understanding.

And understanding preserves what battles alone cannot.

Biblical Markers of Warfare Wisdom

Warfare wisdom is revealed not by the absence of contention, but by how the intercessor carries it. Scripture shows that wisdom does not remove responsibility; it orders it. It teaches the intercessor how to remain engaged without becoming consumed, how to stand without striving, and how to contend without allowing fear, frustration, or reaction to govern posture.

One of the clearest markers of warfare wisdom is discernment of posture. Wisdom teaches when to confront directly and when to stand firmly without escalation. *"The wisdom that is from above is first pure, then peaceable, gentle, willing to yield, full of mercy and good fruits"* **(James 3:17, NKJV)**. This is not passive wisdom; it is disciplined restraint. It understands that authority expressed without love fractures trust, and zeal expressed without patience exhausts the soul.

Another marker is endurance without anxiety. Wisdom steadies the intercessor over time. Scripture says, *"Through wisdom a house is built, and by understanding it is established; by knowledge the rooms are filled"* **(Proverbs 24:3–4, NKJV)**. Wisdom builds what can remain. It does not panic when outcomes are delayed, because it trusts that God's Word is not diminished by time.

Wisdom also guards the intercessor from reactive prayer. It refuses to allow fear to dictate engagement. Jesus demonstrated this repeatedly. Though fully aware of opposition, He did not respond to every provocation. He remained anchored in the Father's will, teaching that wisdom knows when silence preserves authority and when speech establishes order (Matthew 26:63; John 7:6).

Perhaps one of the most personal and enduring expressions of warfare wisdom is seen in the area of family and generational intercession.

In my own life, warfare has not ceased simply because wisdom has grown. I still contend. I still stand in the gap. I still remain watchful, especially concerning my children. Scripture says: *"The enemy desires to sift"* **(Luke 22:31, NKJV)**. That reality does not disappear with maturity. What changes is posture.

Wisdom has taught me NOT to war for my children from fear, judgment, doubt, or worry. Those postures weaken authority rather than strengthen it. Instead, wisdom has trained me to stand in readiness, patience, and love. I learned that anxiety does not accelerate God's promises, and suspicion does not protect destiny. Trust does.

Years ago, I declared and I still declare to this day:
"As for me and my house, we will serve the Lord" **(Joshua 24:15, NKJV).**

That declaration was not made in a moment of emotional urgency. It was spoken from covenant confidence. It was not dependent on my children's age, location, or present behavior. It was anchored in the faithfulness of God. My children are adults now, however, whether they live with me or not, whether they are walking in full alignment or still in process, God's Word remains true.

Warfare wisdom understands this: authority does not fluctuate with circumstances. God's promises do not weaken with time. Faith does not expire because fulfillment appears delayed. *"Let God be true and every man a liar"* **(Romans 3:4, NKJV)**. Wisdom stands on that truth quietly, firmly, and consistently.

This kind of wisdom does not abandon intercession, it sustains it. It teaches the intercessor how to pray with expectancy rather than desperation, how to watch without suspicion, and how to trust God's hand even when the path unfolds slowly.

Warfare continues.
But wisdom governs how it is carried.

The intercessor no longer asks, *"How hard must I fight?"*
They discern, *"How faithfully must I stand?"*

And that wisdom preserves both authority and heart.

The Wisdom Gained Through Warfare

Warfare wisdom is not only learned through Scripture; it is distilled through experience. What the intercessor has endured becomes instruction when it is surrendered to God. Nothing faced in warfare is meant to be wasted. Pain does not disqualify authority, it refines it. What once threatened to overwhelm can now serve as a source of discernment, stability, and depth.

The enemy often attempts to keep intercessors locked in the abyss of what happened, replaying wounds, magnifying loss, and tethering identity to pain rather than purpose. But wisdom refuses that captivity. Wisdom recognizes that survival was not accidental. Endurance was not random. Every season of warfare carried within it the seeds of understanding meant to mature authority.

This is the moment for the intercessor to arise, not from emotion, but from alignment. Not from reaction, but from revelation. Wisdom calls the intercessor out of paralysis and back into posture. It teaches how to stand again without judgment, without doubt, and without worry, anchored instead in patience, love, and trust in God's Word.

Strength must now flow inward before it manifests outward. The inner man must be reinforced. The mind must be steadied. Authority cannot be carried by a fractured interior. God restores alignment so that wisdom governs what warfare once disrupted.

Let what you endured now instruct how you stand.
Let what you survived now inform how you pray.
Let what once wounded now witness to God's faithfulness.

This is not the hour to retreat into memory.
This is the hour to extract wisdom.

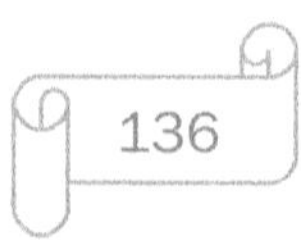

What you have been through does not define you, but it has prepared you. And wisdom ensures that what you carry now is steady, sound, and sustainable.

Warfare continues, because calling continues.
But wisdom now governs how it is carried.

And with that wisdom, the intercessor is prepared to move forward, not merely surviving conflict, but walking toward the stability and authority that follow it.

Prayer

Father,
Thank You for the wisdom You have formed through every season of warfare.
I acknowledge that nothing I endured was wasted in Your hands.

Where battles once required intensity,
teach me now to walk in understanding.
Where pressure once governed my posture,
let wisdom now establish peace.

Strengthen my inner man.
Stabilize my mind.
Restore alignment where weariness tried to distort perspective.

I release the need to remain in survival mode.
I receive Your invitation to stand established, not exhausted.
Prepare me to steward what You have already secured.

Lead me forward with clarity and restraint,
that I may carry authority without striving
and walk in obedience without fear.

Amen.

Declaration

I declare that wisdom now governs warfare.

- I extract understanding from what I have endured.

- I refuse to remain bound to the memory of past battles.

- I stand aligned, restored, and strengthened in my inner man.

- I engage warfare with discernment, not reaction.

- I carry authority with patience, love, and trust in God's Word.

- I move forward established—not exhausted.

What once tested me has trained me.
What I survived has refined my authority.
I walk forward with wisdom.

Reader Reflection

(Journal or meditate prayerfully)

Take a moment to consider these questions before the Lord:

- What wisdom has God formed in me through the battles I've endured?

- Am I still fighting from survival, or am I ready to steward from stability?

- Where might God be inviting me to release old postures shaped by pain or pressure?

- What would it look like to trust that some warfare has already accomplished its purpose?

Do not rush this reflection.
Wisdom settles when it is allowed to be acknowledged.

What you have walked through has not disqualified you.
It has prepared you.

And with wisdom now established, you are ready to move forward—
from warfare into dominion.

Chapter 12: From Warfare to Dominion
Interceding for Nations

Dominion: Authority Settled Into Stewardship

To understand dominion, it must first be defined biblically, not culturally, not politically, and not triumphalistically (Means to act or speak as if victory is exaggerated, self-glorifying, boastful, or dismissive of process, suffering, or humility). In Scripture, dominion is not domination. It is not control, force, or conquest for personal gain. Dominion is authority exercised under God's order, for God's purposes, through stewardship rather than aggression.

The Hebrew word most often translated as *dominion* is **radah** (רָדָה). It means *to rule, govern, tread, or exercise authority*, but always within the context of responsibility. Radah carries the idea of oversight with accountability. It is authority that maintains order, protects what has been entrusted, and ensures alignment with divine intent.

This is why dominion was humanity's original mandate. *"Then God said, 'Let Us make man in Our image... let them have dominion'"* **(Genesis 1:26, NKJV)**. Dominion preceded warfare. Humanity was not created to live in constant battle, but to steward creation in partnership with God. Warfare entered the story because dominion was contested, not because it was abandoned. God's redemptive work restores dominion, not as unchecked power, but as aligned authority.

For the intercessor, dominion represents the maturation of prayer. It is the place where authority no longer reacts to resistance but maintains what has been established. Prayer shifts from contending to governing, from breakthrough to preservation, from survival to stewardship.

Two biblical lives clearly illustrate this transition.

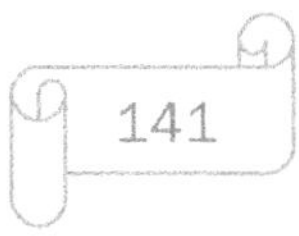

Joseph: Dominion Through Faithful Stewardship

Joseph's journey began in warfare—betrayal, injustice, false accusation, and prolonged waiting. Yet Scripture records that Joseph did not fight every injustice he faced. Instead, he remained faithful within each assignment God placed before him. Over time, warfare refined his character, discernment, and restraint.

When dominion arrived, it came quietly. Pharaoh said, *"You shall be over my house, and all my people shall be ruled according to your word"* **(Genesis 41:40, NKJV)**. Joseph did not seize authority; it was entrusted to him. His dominion was expressed not through force, but through wisdom, administration, and foresight. He governed resources, preserved nations, and sustained generations during famine.

Joseph's authority did not eliminate hardship, it created order in the midst of it. This is dominion. The intercessor learns that authority proven in hidden warfare becomes stewardship entrusted in visible responsibility.

Solomon: Dominion Established Through Wisdom

Solomon inherited a kingdom stabilized by David's warfare. Scripture notes that *"the Lord gave Solomon wisdom and exceedingly great understanding"* **(1Kings 4:29, NKJV)**. Solomon's dominion was marked not by constant battle, but by governance, peace, and order. Nations came not to challenge him, but to learn from him.

Yet Solomon's life also offers a caution. Dominion requires ongoing alignment. Wisdom sustains authority only when it remains submitted to God. Solomon's later compromises demonstrate that dominion is not self-maintaining. Authority must be continually stewarded. Dominion does not mean the intercessor disengages from vigilance; it means vigilance is now exercised through obedience rather than warfare.

Together, these examples reveal dominion's true nature: authority settled into responsibility. Dominion does not remove the need for prayer; it changes its function. Prayer now preserves alignment, guards stewardship, and sustains what God has entrusted.

For the intercessor, dominion is not a finish line, it is a posture. It is the place where prayer governs rather than reacts, where authority remains steady rather than strained, and where God's purposes are maintained over time.

Warfare taught you how to stand.
Wisdom taught you how to remain.
Dominion teaches you how to steward.

And from this posture, the intercessor is prepared to stand, not only for personal or territorial matters, but for the unfolding purposes of God among nations.

Interceding for Nations: Dominion Extended Beyond the Self

When dominion is established, authority does not retreat inward, it is released outward. Scripture shows that national intercession is not assigned to those still fighting for personal survival, but to those who have learned how to steward authority with restraint. Nations are not shaped by intensity; they are shifted through faithful, sustained alignment with God's purposes.

Interceding for nations requires a different posture than personal warfare. It demands patience, discernment, and long obedience. National strongholds are layered, historical, and often maintained through systems rather than individuals. The intercessor who stands for nations must be grounded enough to contend without being consumed and discerning enough to engage without reaction.

Two lives in Scripture clearly reveal what national intercession looks like when dominion and wisdom are present.

Daniel: Interceding Through Alignment and Longevity

Daniel did not enter Babylon as a warrior; he entered as a captive. Yet his authority was not diminished by displacement. Over decades of exile, shifting empires, and changing rulers, Daniel remained aligned. His intercession was marked by consistency rather than confrontation.

When Daniel prayed for his nation, he did so with historical awareness and covenant responsibility. He understood why Israel was in exile and did not pray defensively or accusatorily. Instead, he prayed with humility, confession, and alignment with God's Word:

"We have sinned and committed iniquity... therefore the curse and the oath written in the Law of Moses... have been poured out on us" **(Daniel 9:5, 11, NKJV)**.

Daniel's prayer did not demand immediate reversal. It is acknowledged process. He prayed from understanding, not urgency. This is warfare wisdom applied at a national level, recognizing that some outcomes unfold through time, repentance, and realignment rather than instant deliverance.

Daniel's authority was not loud, but it was enduring. He influenced kings, preserved prophetic truth, and stood through generations. This is dominion expressed through faithfulness. The intercessor learns that nations are often shaped not by dramatic moments, but by those who remain aligned when others compromise.

Esther: Interceding Through Courageous Positioning

Esther's intercession reveals another essential dimension of national authority: positioning. At first, she did not fully recognize the weight of where she had been placed. It was Mordecai's words that awakened her to responsibility:
"Yet who knows whether you have come to the kingdom for such a time as this?" **(Esther 4:14, NKJV)**.

This moment marks the shift from awareness to accountability. Esther realized that her position was not incidental, it was intentional. Authority had been granted not for personal elevation, but for intercession on behalf of a people.

Her response is striking. Esther's intercession did not begin with public prayer or immediate action. It began with fasting, humility, and alignment. Before approaching the king, she prepared herself spiritually, understanding that authority exercised without wisdom could cost her life. Her courage was not impulsive; it was measured. She recognized that timing mattered as much as obedience.

Esther did not confront systems loudly or argue policy publicly. She interceded from *within* her assigned position, trusting God to move hearts and reverse decrees. Her warfare was marked by restraint, discernment, and obedience. God may assign different strategies to confront systems, but the intercessor's responsibility remains the same: to obey the instruction given.

The deliverance of a nation flowed not from noise, but from submission, quiet courage carried faithfully until the moment of action arrived.

Esther's warfare also reveals why fasting matters in intercession. She was not confronting a personal inconvenience, but a decree written against an entire people, enforced by law and sustained by power. This required more than bravery; it required alignment. Esther's fast was not an attempt to persuade God, but a means of positioning herself and the people before engaging authority. Fasting clarified timing, quieted fear, and stripped personal impulse so that when she spoke, her words carried consequence rather than emotion.

In the warfare of an intercessor, fasting often marks the transition from awareness to authorized confrontation. It steadies the intercessor before engagement, ensuring that resistance is met with discernment rather than urgency. Esther's victory did not begin when she spoke, it began when she aligned.

The Pattern for the Intercessor

Daniel and Esther reveal the same truth through different paths: national intercession flows from dominion, not desperation. It requires maturity that can carry delayed outcomes and wisdom that knows when to speak, when to fast, and when to wait.

Interceding for nations is not about controlling outcomes or forcing change. It is about standing in alignment with God's redemptive purposes over peoples, systems, and generations. The intercessor becomes aware that their prayers participate in shaping history, not quickly, but faithfully.

This is the final extension of the intercessor's journey. Authority that has been refined through warfare and stabilized through wisdom is now entrusted with broader responsibility. The intercessor stands not as one reacting to crisis, but as one partnering with Heaven for long-term transformation.

Dominion prepares the intercessor to remain.
Wisdom teaches them how to endure.
And national intercession invites them to stand
not for a moment, but for generations.

Regional Intercession

By the time Paul's voice emerges in Scripture, the pattern of apostolic intercession is already established. He does not introduce a new model; he confirms one. Paul's life demonstrates that regional intercession is not driven by emotion, crisis, or visibility, but by assignment recognized and sustained over time.

Paul consistently spoke of regions entrusted to him not as territory he conquered, but as responsibility he stewarded. His language reveals awareness of spiritual jurisdiction, boundaries set by God, and restraint shaped by obedience. Where he went, where he remained, and where he refrained were all governed by divine instruction, not personal preference.

This confirms a critical truth for the intercessor:
regional authority is not assumed, it is assigned.

Paul did not attempt to carry every burden or address every issue. He understood that authority expands only where alignment is preserved. His earlier prayers for maturity, endurance, and revelation now reveal their purpose they stabilized regions so that the work could remain after his departure.

In this way, Paul's apostolic intercession complements the models of Daniel and Esther rather than repeating them. Daniel reveals longevity across empires. Esther reveals positioning within systems. Paul confirms the necessity of sustained stewardship across regions, where prayer continues long after presence ends.

Regional intercession, then, is not defined by constant engagement. It is defined by faithfulness to assignment. The intercessor learns to pray in ways that reinforce order, protect alignment, and prepare others to carry responsibility forward.

This is where dominion quietly expands.

Authority that has been refined through warfare and governed by wisdom does not remain static. It is extended carefully, deliberately, and responsibly, into cities, regions, and ultimately nations. The intercessor no longer measures effectiveness by immediate change, but by what remains aligned over time.

Paul's life reminds us that apostolic intercession is not loud, hurried, or everywhere at once.
It is faithful, restrained, and enduring.

And it confirms what this chapter has been building toward all along:

Dominion is not the end of intercession.
It is the posture from which intercession is sent.

**Warfare does not conclude when dominion is established.
It transitions from engagement to governance.**

There will always be resistance in the earth. Kingdom authority is not measured by the absence of conflict, but by the ability to rule within it. Dominion is the posture of one who no longer reacts to opposition but governs in alignment with Heaven's order.

This is the movement Scripture reveals, from warfare to dominion.

Dominion is not conquest. It is stewardship. It is authority exercised without haste, restraint maintained without fear, and responsibility carried without display. It is the ability to hold territory once it has been secured, to keep what God has established from drifting, and to remain aligned when pressure no longer announces itself loudly.

As dominion settles, jurisdiction expands.

The intercessor who has been formed through personal warfare is now entrusted with broader responsibility. Prayer is no longer confined to just personal need or immediate environment. It begins to take on governmental weight standing in the gap for families, cities, systems, and nations. This is not ambition; it is entrustment.

Interceding for nations does not always look like public declaration or visible influence. Often, it looks like sustained alignment over time, praying in obscurity, standing in agreement with God's purposes when outcomes unfold slowly, and remaining faithful when history is still being written. National intercession is less about controlling outcomes and more about enforcing covenantal order.

Warfare remains present. Dominion governs how it is engaged. Authority remains active. Wisdom governs how it is exercised.

The intercessor does not lay down prayer, they lay down striving.
They do not disengage from conflict; they steward it.
They do not abandon the earth, they stand within it as representatives of Heaven's government.

This is the posture of apostolic intercession, to rule without domination, to contend without exhaustion,
and to steward authority without losing alignment.

As you close this book, you are not released from responsibility.
You are commissioned into it, quietly, firmly, and without spectacle.

From warfare to dominion.
From personal formation to national responsibility.
From contending to governing.

This is the work of the intercessor who remains.

Prayer

Righteous Judge and Governor of all the earth,
I yield myself to Your authority and Your purposes.
Teach me to steward what You have established
with wisdom, restraint, and faithfulness.
Align my prayers with Heaven's government
and entrust me with responsibility beyond myself.

Let Your will be enforced in the earth through obedience.
Amen.

Declaration

- I declare that I am aligned with Heaven's government.

- I steward authority with wisdom and restraint.

- I stand in the gap for families, regions, and nations.

- What God has established, I will guard and govern faithfully.

- I remain submitted, watchful, and obedient.

Reader Reflection

(Journal or meditate prayerfully)

As you receive this commissioning, pause and consider:

- What authority has God entrusted to me, not to display, but to steward?

- What territory, personal, generational, regional, or national, has Heaven placed under my watch?

- How might my posture shift if I viewed obedience as governance rather than effort?

- What would it look like to stand at my post without striving for recognition or release?

Allow these questions to settle. Commissioning is not proven by immediate action, but by sustained alignment. Let clarity form before movement and let responsibility be carried with peace.

You are not being asked to do more.
You are being entrusted to remain.

Healing Prayer for the Intercessor

Father God,

I come before You on behalf of every intercessor who endured battles they did not understand, carried weight they could not name, and survived warfare they never volunteered for. You saw every season of confusion, every unanswered question, every moment when resistance felt personal and unexplained. Nothing was wasted, and nothing escaped Your attention.

I ask now that You heal what was bruised in the process of building.
Restore the places that were strengthened under pressure but never tended afterward. Heal the heart that learned endurance before it learned rest. Heal the mind that stayed alert for danger but forgot how to exhale. Heal the spirit that stood faithfully while silently absorbing the cost of obedience.

Lord, reveal gently but clearly that the warfare was not punishment, nor abandonment, nor delay. It was preparation. What felt like opposition was often shaping. What felt like loss was often refinement. What felt like isolation was sometimes protection. Remove every false narrative that the enemy attached to the pain lies of failure, inadequacy, abandonment, or disqualification.

I ask that You now release healing without resistance.
Let peace settle where vigilance once lived.
Let joy return where sorrow lingered too long.
Let hope rise where discouragement attempted to take root.

I declare that the intercessor is not broken, they are built.
They are not delayed, they are established.
They are not weakened, they are strengthened through wisdom.

Where trauma tried to define identity, I ask You to restore truth.
Where disappointment tried to narrow vision, expand it again.
Where grief tried to silence prayer, let authority be renewed.

Father, anchor them now not in survival, but in governance.
Let them see clearly that what they endured was shaping capacity, not diminishing value. Strengthen them from the inside out. Restore emotional range, spiritual confidence, and relational trust. Heal what was carried too long without explanation.

And now, Lord, seal the work You have done in them.
Let their past no longer drain them, but inform them.
Let their history no longer accuse them, but serve them.
Let the residue of old seasons lift, and let clarity take its place.

I bless the intercessor with rest that does not compromise readiness,
peace that does not weaken authority,
and healing that strengthens future obedience.

What was built through warfare, You now establish through healing.

In Jesus' name,
Amen.

A Prayer of Restoration and Return
(Prayer Life)

Father God,

I come before You on behalf of every son and daughter whose heart has quietly drifted, whose prayer life has grown silent, and whose calling feels distant. You have not been surprised by the distance, nor offended by the weariness. You have watched patiently, not with disappointment, but with longing.

Lord, we acknowledge that the drifting did not happen in a moment. It happened through disappointment, unanswered prayers, prolonged warfare, unmet expectations, and wounds that went unattended. Some did not walk away in rebellion, but in exhaustion. Some did not abandon You, but slowly closed their heart to protect it.

Today, we bring all of it into Your light.

Father, forgive where discouragement hardened into distance.
Forgive where silence replaced trust.
Forgive where self-protection replaced surrender.

Not with shame, but with mercy.

I ask now that You restore first love, not emotional excitement, but covenant devotion. Rekindle desire for Your presence where prayer once felt heavy. Awaken hunger where routine replaced relationship. Let the heart feel again what it tried to numb in order to survive.

Lord, breathe again on dormant calling.
What was buried under disappointment, uncover gently.
What was laid down in grief, lift without pressure.
What was silenced by fear, restore with confidence.

Break the lie that says it is too late.
Break the lie that says they forfeited their assignment.
Break the lie that says distance disqualifies.

Your Word declares that You restore the soul. You are the God who brings back, renews, and rebuilds what seemed lost. Where prayer has been absent, let grace reintroduce conversation. Where obedience has felt costly, let trust be renewed.

I declare that this is not a return to striving, but a return to alignment. Not a return to pressure, but to presence. Not a return to obligation, but to identity.

Father meet them where they are—without accusation, without delay. Let them know that You never withdrew calling, never revoked purpose, never stopped watching the door.

We say yes again—not because we are strong, but because You are faithful.

Restore hearts.
Restore prayer.
Restore calling.

In Jesus' name,
Amen.

A Prayer of Repentance and Realignment

Father God,

I come before You with humility and truth. I acknowledge that there were moments when I drew back, not because I stopped loving You, but because the warfare became overwhelming. I confess that weariness, disappointment, and prolonged resistance caused me to retreat in places where You had called me to stand.

Forgive me, Lord, for withdrawing my heart when it needed healing.
Forgive me for silencing my prayer when it needed rest.
Forgive me for stepping back from obedience out of fatigue rather than trust.

I repent, not with shame, but with clarity.
I repent of allowing discouragement to speak louder than truth.
I repent of letting fear, confusion, or unanswered questions interrupt my posture of faith.
I repent of agreeing with the lie that stepping away was safer than remaining aligned.

Lord, cleanse my heart from any residue of bitterness, self-protection, or doubt that formed during that season. Where I guarded myself instead of trusting You, I ask for restoration. Where I chose distance instead of dependence, I ask for renewal.

I thank You that repentance does not disqualify me, it realigns me.
I thank You that You are not offended by my honesty, nor distant because of my weakness.
I thank You that Your mercy meets me here, fully and completely.

Today, I turn my heart back toward You.
I return to prayer, not striving but trusting.
I return to obedience, not pressured, but willing.
I return to my calling, not burdened, but restored.

Reestablish my footing, Lord.
Heal what the warfare strained.
Strengthen what fatigue weakened.
Restore my confidence in Your faithfulness.

I receive Your grace afresh.
I receive alignment without condemnation.
I receive the assurance that You never withdrew Your hand from me, even when I stepped back.

I choose to stand again, not in my own strength, but in Yours.

In Jesus' name,
Amen.

A Gentle Altar Moment

If you sense the Holy Spirit drawing you, pause here.

This is not a call to explain where you've been or defend why you drifted. It is simply an invitation to return, to bring your heart back into alignment without fear of judgment or expectation.

You do not need to feel emotional.
You do not need perfect words.
You do not need to promise more than you can give.

Simply offer your willingness.

If you are able, place your hand over your heart and whisper,
"Lord, here I am."
Let that be enough.

God is not measuring how far you wandered, He is honoring that you turned back. He is not reopening past failures; He is restoring present alignment. The altar is not a place of shame; it is a place of exchange.

Receive His mercy.
Receive His nearness.
Receive the quiet assurance that calling is still intact.

When you are ready, rise in peace.
You have not been disqualified.
You have been welcomed home.

Glory to God! He loves you with an everlasting love dear heart!
Now go back to the Introduction of this book and re read
"Commissioning Declaration for Apostolic Intercessors".

Scripture Index by Chapter

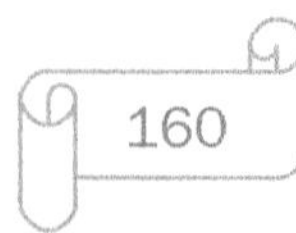

* Matthew 12:29

Chapter 10 – The Commissioned Intercessor
* John 20:21
* Luke 12:48
* 1 Corinthians 4:1–2
* Jeremiah 1:7–10
* Isaiah 6:6–8

Chapter 11 – Warfare Wisdom
* Isaiah 40:31
* Ecclesiastes 7:8
* James 1:2–5
* Hebrews 12:11
* Joshua 24:15

Chapter 12 – From Warfare to Dominion: Interceding for Nations
* Genesis 1:26–28
* Daniel 9
* Esther 4:14–17
* Psalm 2:8
* 1 Timothy 2:1–4
* Habakkuk 2:14

Glossary of Key Terms

Alignment

The state of being positioned in agreement with God's will, timing, and instruction. Alignment precedes authority and determines effectiveness in prayer.

Apostolic Intercession

Is prayer that flows from being sent with divine authority. It is assignment-based rather than reactive, aligned with Heaven's purposes rather than circumstances. Rooted in the prayer life of the apostles in the New Testament, this form of intercession does not merely respond to need, but establishes, strengthens, and governs the Church according to God's will.

Assignment

A divinely given responsibility or sphere of engagement entrusted to an intercessor. Not every burden discerned is an assignment given.

Authority

Delegated power granted by God to enforce His will in the earth. Authority operates through obedience, not volume or emotion.

Carrier

An intercessor entrusted to bear spiritual weight revelation, burden, or responsibility on behalf of others, regions, or systems.

Commissioning

The moment Heaven entrusts authority and responsibility after formation is complete. Commissioning follows readiness, not calling alone.

Confrontation

Intentional, authorized engagement with resistance or strongholds. Biblical confrontation is measured, obedient, and governed by wisdom.

Consequential Prayer

Prayer that carries long-term impact and responsibility. Unlike urgent prayer, it governs what remains after God moves.

Discernment

Spiritual perception developed through maturity and obedience, enabling the intercessor to recognize what to confront, endure, or ignore.

Dominion

Responsible stewardship and governance under God's authority. Dominion is not domination, but authority settled into order. It means to rule, subjugate, to tread down, to reign, to have dominion.

Endurance

Faithful persistence without striving. Endurance sustains alignment during prolonged warfare or delayed manifestation.

Establishing Territory

The act of stewarding what God has promised or released so it remains aligned, protected, and productive over time.

Friendly Fire

Spiritual or relational damage caused within the ranks, often through prolonged warfare, misalignment, or lack of wisdom rather than demonic attack.

Governance

The mature exercise of authority that maintains order, alignment, and stability after breakthrough has occurred.

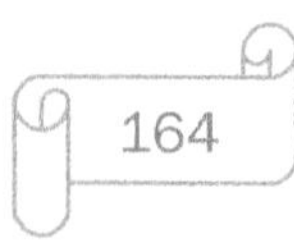

Intercession

Standing in the gap on behalf of others, systems, or purposes to align earth with Heaven's will.

Mandate

A divine authorization that defines responsibility rather than option. Warfare as a mandate means intercession is vocational, not occasional.

Precision

Accuracy in prayer, praying what God has authorized, at the right time, in the right manner.

Prophetic Intercession

Prayer informed by revelation from God, discerning His intent before engaging resistance or declaring outcomes.

Refilling

The divine restoration of strength, clarity, peace, and capacity after seasons of pouring out or warfare.

Residue

Emotional, spiritual, or mental weight left behind from prolonged warfare that must be healed or released.

Restraint

Wisdom-governed authority that knows when *not* to engage. Restraint protects both the intercessor and the assignment.

Strategic Prayer

Intentional, discerning prayer aligned with Heaven's blueprint. Strategic prayer governs engagement rather than reacting to pressure.

Stronghold

Entrenched resistance, personal or systemic, that sustains opposition against God's will through longevity rather than intensity.

Sustaining the Fire

Maintaining spiritual vitality without burnout through obedience, rhythm, rest, and reliance on God.

Warfare

The spiritual conflict that arises in response to divine assignments. Biblical warfare is governed, intentional, and authoritative.

Warfare Wisdom

Discernment gained through endured battles, producing maturity rather than trauma.

Apostolic Commissioning and Sending

Having been formed through warfare, instructed by truth, and stabilized through wisdom, you are now released, not merely to pray, but to govern. This is not an invitation; it is a sending. You are not commissioned by emotion, experience, or ambition, but by alignment with Heaven's authority.

By the authority of Jesus Christ, the Head of the Church, and in agreement with Heaven's government, you are sent as an intercessor entrusted with jurisdiction. You are commissioned to enforce what God has decreed, to confront what resists His will, and to steward what He establishes in the earth. You are authorized to stand within your assigned sphere, family, church, region, or nation, and to legislate through prayer and intercession according to Heaven's order.

This commissioning marks a shift from engagement to governance. You are no longer merely responding to burden; you are responsible for outcome. Your prayers are now weighed, measured, and consequential. What you bind and loose must remain aligned with Heaven's will, for authority exercised outside of alignment does not endure.

You are sent to pray with precision, to contend with restraint, and to remain immovable under pressure. You are not authorized to engage every battle you discern, but you are accountable for the ones Heaven assigns. You are sent to establish order where chaos has lingered, to dismantle strongholds through obedience, and to guard territory once it has been secured.

This is a legislative calling. Your intercession participates in Heaven's rulings. Your obedience enforces Heaven's verdicts. Your endurance sustains what God intends to remain. Fire will stay on your altar, not through striving, but through holy order.

Go forth, therefore, as a sent one. Govern wisely. Remain submitted. Enforce faithfully. Heaven has entrusted you with authority because you have been prepared to steward it.

You are sent.

Author's Closing

This book was written from lived ground. Not from theory, but from seasons where prayer was tested, endurance was required, and alignment mattered more than outcome. My love for prayer began the moment I was born again over 20 years ago and over time it became more than devotion it became assignment. For more than fourteen years, I stewarded a prayer ministry in Chicago, IL under the leadership of Apostle Marlon Hester of GWMI. I carried the responsibility of intercession, leadership, and Small Groups. I have also been entrusted with my own prayer ministry, and I have taught, activated, and trained intercessors to pray with clarity, authority, and restraint.

 I wrote these pages for those who have learned, often the hard way that warfare is not a moment you pass through, but a calling you grow into. This is a path I know well, not only because I have taught it, but because I have lived it. If you recognize yourself here, it is because the resistance you faced was never accidental. Much of what you endured was aimed at delaying your obedience, dulling your discernment, or persuading you to step back when Heaven had already positioned you to stand. I know that weight personally. I also know that what survives warfare emerges with clarity.

I want you to know this: nothing you have carried was wasted. Even the seasons that felt confusing, heavy, or unproductive were shaping posture, not punishing faith. What once felt like opposition was often preparation, forming restraint, sharpening wisdom, and anchoring you more deeply in God than ease ever could.

I release you from this book not with urgency, but with trust. You are not sent to strive harder, but to govern more wisely. Let prayer remain your language, alignment your foundation, and obedience your measure of success. May what you have learned here continue to steady you long after these pages close.

And when warfare rises again as it will, may you remember that you were never called merely to endure it, but to steward what Heaven has entrusted to you.

With care and conviction,

Sabrina